Author's Notes

My 24 years of Mushing Experiences include numerous distance races and 22 years as Owner/Operator of Dogsled Express - Winter-Guided Sled Dog Tours, Mount Shasta, California. I currently manage a kennel of over 70 Alaskan Huskies. My qualifications include: Chairperson of the Siskiyou Snow Dogs: Organizer of the Siskiyou Sled Dog Races: Proud recipient of the Veterinarian's Award of "Best Keep Team" at Washington State's Cascade Quest 220-Mile Sled Dog Race,2004: Sportsmanship Awards at the Atta Boy 300, Race to the Sky 350 and Cascade Quest 220.

Recently a poem spoke to me. It goes like this.

> Dogs don't lie, and why should I?
> Strangers come, and they bark,
> They know their loved ones in the dark.
> Now let me by night or day,
> Be just as full of truth as they.

My goal while writing this book was to be like the dogs in the poem above. To be truthful and honest to the reader of the thoughts and emotions I experienced while competing in an actual 220 mile sled dog race.

I want my readers to see the love, respect and deep bond that the dog driver and dogs develop over a lifetime on the trail. To get a feel of the quiet language spoken through the lines off the team. Most importantly I want you to experience the courage and determination that the sled dogs posses. They are the ultimate adventurers.

This story is written in both the voice of lead dog Casper and dog driver Pat, giving the reader a unique insight into the sport of sled dog distance racing, thoughts and emotions shared by both man and canine when matched against the elements of Mother Nature.

What starts out as a simple sled dog race quickly turns into something so much more for both Pat and his canine buddies and you the reader. I hope you enjoy the ride with both the highs and the lows of being out on the trail that "Song of The Runners", will take you on.

S0-CGP-125

Acknowledgments:

First and foremost to my loving wife and editor, Lisa, who continues to believe in me as a writer, a person, a husband. Her support inspires me to better myself on so many levels. I love you Lisa.

Thanks to a special lady from Livingston Texas who is our biggest literary fan and also helped with editing and encouraged us to get this into publication....My mother-in law, Joy Wright

Of course I need to thank Casper and the dogs for their courage, determination and lessons they teach us. To live each day to your best, and love life, no matter what cards life has dealt you.

A special thanks to my Mom and Dad, (Eileen and Soup Campbell) who I owe so much. Years ago my Father wrote in a journal before he passed on, that he thought I would be a writer some day! He is right once again.

Thanks to all the mushers that I had the honor of competing against at the Siskiyou 2009 Sled Dog Races. They all performed with such class a sportsmanship, despite all the challenges of the trail.

The volunteers at the Siskiyou Sled Dog Races did such an outstanding job. The support, foods etc. at the Start/Finish Line and checkpoints were as organized as I have ever seen. Special thanks to Bill Daugereau (distance race marshal) and Allen Iverson (sprint race marshal).

Often at sled dog races the least appreciated and least noticed are the race veterinarians. Dr. Doug Marks and Dr. Erica McKenzie did an outstanding job administering their skills and sled dog care, giving each dog racing the medical support to compete at their highest level.

Song of the Runners

"Story told by

Musher Pat and Lead Dog Casper"

Written By/Pat Campbell

11/5/2012

Based on true experiences at the

"Siskiyou 220 Mile Iditarod Qualifier Sled Dog Race", 2009

Table of Contents

Authors Notes   1

Acknowledgements   2

Title Page   3

Table of Contents   4

Pre-Race   5

Trouble On The Trail   10

The Team   24

Laugh It Up   35

Dog Care   44

We're Going To Finish This Race   61

Race To The Finish   67

Two Evenings Later   81

THE PRE-RACE

While lying in bed, the slow tick of the alarm clock keeps me awake. 3 am. Booties. Meat snacks. Headlamp batteries. Musher's meeting. How much did it rain on the trail yesterday? The list of things I need to check and double check, keep racing through my head. Sure wish I could turn it off so I could get a little more sleep.

My mind drifts to the challenges ahead for me and my dogs (my kids). They'll be put to the test as never before. They have no idea how different the next couple of days will be for them. Are they ready for 220 miles in two days? Will the young dogs know how to settle down and get their needed rest early in the race? I start to question myself as to why we are even doing this. Every distance musher goes through this doubt process-at least I'd like to think so. I hope it isn't just me! Ahh, just relax Pat. Enjoy the weekend, the trail, the dogs and your fellow mushers. I know I have one thing in common with them all, they have to be just as crazy as I am.

I remind myself that if we stick to our goals, it will be a good race. Pay attention to the dogs' attitudes and run the best race we can. Seize and enjoy each moment. Be patient-with the race, the elements and the dogs. Above all, put the dogs and dog care first. Take care of them and they will take care of me. We will do our best to finish and not worry about where we are in the standings. Next thing I remember, the alarm clock is going off. It's time to do this thing.

Casper:

The lights come on in the log cabin where my best friends Pat and Lisa live. I lift a leg and a stretch as Rupert starts the kennel's morning song. A good howl is always the right way to start the day. Pat is on schedule, filling the buckets full of water for us to drink between giving sled rides. As he starts to load up my pals into the trailer I see that he is only taking a few of us. Maybe we have a light day at work? I'd better show my excitement so that he'll pick me! "Bark, bark, spin, bark, jump, bark!".."Don't worry Casper, you get to go today," Pat smiles. I can relax now; I get to go! I see that he is taking only fast dogs. We haven't gotten to run together for at least a moon cycle. I wonder, what's up? When Pat gets to me, he kneels down, looks deep into my eyes and says, "I'm counting on you Casper, I really need you, I love you, now let's go have some fun"! I love you too, but what the heck is he talking about? We always have fun when we run. Oh well, time will tell. I arrange the wood chips in my dog box and settle into a nice little nap on the way to the trailhead.

Sniff, sniff. Is that a Juniper tree I smell? Junipers! We aren't going to the ski park trail to give sled rides. We're going to our old trail at Deer Mountain. Oh boy! When was the last time I ran this trail? It must have been around four winters ago. My Gosh, it was the weekend that we ran in that race! Are we going to a race? Bark, bark, "Hey you guys wake up! We might be going to a race today!" "What's a race?" "Yeah, what's a race?' "Well, you rookies, we might get to go run on new trails and compete against other dog teams from all over the countryside. We're almost there so we'll know soon."

There they are. Just look at all the dog trucks and people. Is that a beautiful sight or what? Bark. "Hey you guys, we get to race, WHOOHOO!

Boy did that get all my pals excited. I'm gonna have my paws full, leading all these young boys and girls! I can't wait! "Arrhaa. Arrhaa. Hurry up Pat."

Pat:

Well, there they are. Dog trucks ahead and a dog truck following me. Hard to believe the race is really going to happen. Two years of planning. Last year we were ready, when a huge windstorm blew in, downing trees and blocking the trails, so we had to cancel the race.

Where's my list of things to do? Here it is! Let's see…Get the dogs out and watered before their examination by the veterinarians. Explain to the volunteers the set up we need for the start line. Call the mushers' meeting, and introduce the vets and Bill Daugereau, our race marshal. Explain about the trail, the terrain, and the bare spots where the snow has melted off. Give a weather report. Pack the sled with the mandatory gear. Pack the drop bags that are going to the checkpoints and get them to the drop bag trucks.

All right! The snow at the trailhead looks better than I thought it would after those heavy rains we had yesterday. Maybe the snow will come in early tomorrow so the sprint dog teams can use the loop trails instead of the out and back trail. I see the vets are inspecting a dog team already. This is that musher's first vet check and distance race. Stepping up from the sprint circuit where he has done so well. They'll be fast. But will they have the confidence at the half-way point? I need to find a parking spot where we have a straight shot to the starting line. There's one.

Casper:

Wow. Bark. Check out the ladies on that team you guys! I'd better shake off and look my best. Arrhaa. Hurry up Pat. Let me out. I have some flirtation to do here. Finally Pat opens my box door. I spring out. Quick lift of a leg, ahhh, that's better. Now let's show my stuff. Let me see, first a long low stretch. Yah, I've got her attention. Now a couple of circles, a little wag of my tail… work it big boy! "Hey Rupert, look, that cutie over there is checking me out." "She is not, she's checking me out", Rupert says. "She wants nothing to do with you two old boys, she's looking at me, the young stud!" Tipper spouts up. I say "No way. Here, I'll prove it." I give her a little bark, and as she looks back over her shoulder, I show my best smile, a slight wink and a gentle wag of my tail.

She shyly looks away, looks back again and gives me a return wag with a slight sway of her backside. See, I told you guys. "Yah, yah, whatever", as the other boys concede.

"Hey Casper, what are the humans doing to those dogs?" Elizabeth asks. Oh, that is the vet check. They are going to look us all over, from our gums, to see if we are hydrated, to our feet, wrists,

shoulders and even our tail and below, if you know what I mean…
"That is a weird necklace they have on," Patchy says. I tell her, "No
Patchy, that's not a necklace, they use it to listen to our lungs and
heart. They want to make sure you are in good health to go as far as
we are going."

"How far are we going to run Casper?" Preacher asks. "Well
Preacher, that is up to Pat. We have to trust his decision on that.
Hey you guys. This is a big deal, this race. I want everyone at your
best. We have to work as a team to get to the finish line. I don't
want to hear any whining and nobody quits until Pat says it is time to
quit. He is counting on all of us. Are you all with me? "Yip, yip,
we're with you Casper." "Good!" "OK," "Here comes the vet.
Everyone smile and lift your tail!"

We pass with flying colors. I notice Pat checking out the
cute vet with the funny accent as she walks away. Boy, Pat better
hope Lisa doesn't catch him looking at that. I kind of like my dog
house and I don't think it's big enough for the two of us!

Pat:

At last, the vet check is over. All the dogs passed inspection.
The mushers' meeting went well. We're packing sled bags and
preparing drop bags. Where is everything? I can't seem to focus on
simple tasks. Slow down Pat. All of a sudden, I realize how tired I
am. Will I be all right out there? If I'm having trouble now, how
will I be in 24 hours with no sleep and physically exhausted? A
sense of panic is building, when my good buddy, musher and past

dog handler, Rick, walks over. While talking to Rick, I feel my calmness return. I remember my goals for the race and I feel better. There is Lisa, my fiancée. She comes over, gives me a big hug and kiss and all is well again. Let's get booties on these dog's feet and get this show on the trail!

TROUBLE ON THE TRAIL
Race Start and on to Ski Park Checkpoint

Pat:

The ATV and driver approach my sled. The volunteers hook a carbine with a line to the back of the team's centerline, securing the team to the ATV. I give them the "go ahead slow" sign. Great! We get into the starting shoot without a problem. The team is really focused and at attention as I walk alongside them while giving them each a reassuring pat on the head. Casper and I make eye contact. No words need to be spoken. We know what is ahead.

All of a sudden Casper lunges in his harness and the whole team responds. This is it. Casper has fired the engines! Five, four, three, I take off in a dash to the sled. Pull the snow hook and we are off, flying up the trail with spectators on both sides cheering for us…, the local team. Wow, there are a lot of spectators this year! Plus, look at all the photographers leaning out in front of the dogs for the ultimate shot. All right, let's settle down, we have a long ways to go. I stay on the brake for some time, as each dog slowly changes from a lope into a nice steady trot. Many a team has scratched a race because of going too fast in the first leg.

Casper:

Arrah, arrah, come on! Doesn't that machine move any faster than that? Finally, there's the starting line. Unhook us from that stupid machine. Pat! Set us free! Here he comes. He gives us all a little love and encouragement. Let me see. He has Tipper and Elizabeth in the wheel position in front of the sled, then Rupert with his half sister Preacher, the puppy Patchy with Sheenje, then my sister Snowy and her daughter Lady, with Cheena and her sister Panda behind me in the point position and my little girl friend Pudges, beside me in lead.

This is a nice team Pat has put together. I don't see any problems with this twelve dog team setup.

When Pat gets to me, we have one of those old soul moments where we know what each other is thinking. He's concerned about what lies ahead of us with all these young dogs.

Pat's a tough ole bird but I'm concerned for him because he looks so tired. "Don't worry Pat we'll get through this. I'm here for you buddy." I take one step back and slam into the harness. Bark, bark, bark, come on you guys, and look sharp for all these fine folks. Two, one, we're off. Yeah baby, this is what I'm talking about... We're flying! Pat's hard on the brake while talking us down into a nice trot. He's probably right; we'd better take it easy. We have a long way to go.

Pat:

 There is Pomeroy Ridge. Looking over my shoulder, I see a team is coming up fast. Don't worry about them. There will be some small open spots of pavement showing when we head down the other side of the ridge... shouldn't be a problem. We used to give rides here all the time over small open patches of pavement. As we crest the ridge, we see a dog team approaching us! What the heck is going on? It's the team from Washington that has a shot at winning. The musher is on one leg as we approach. "What's the matter?" I yell. As he goes buy he calmly says, "I broke my ankle". "Oh No," was all I could say.

 I know how he feels. The first corner, in my first race in Oregon, I blew my left knee out. There went my whole season in a second!

Casper:

 As we go over the pass, I can tell that something is very wrong. One of those really good-looking teams is coming back toward us. The driver doesn't look right. Pat calls out "Gee" for us to pass on the right, and hollers, "ON BY!" Something looks wrong with the musher's ankle and his dogs whisper to me to stay on the right side. What did they say? Stay to the right... why? I always run down the middle of the trail. Wow, now that is an open patch of pavement. There is some snow over on the left. We'll head over there. Pat likes it when we keep the sled on the snow.

Pat:

OH NO! Look at the size of that open patch of pavement! Not good! As we approach the open spot, Casper heads the team to the left where there is a narrow trail of snow. "No, straight ahead Casper," I shout. He's not paying attention. There is snow over there and that's where he is headed. All of a sudden the sled starts to slide sideways. This has never happened to me here before. I guess the weight of the passengers in the sled always kept us going straight. By the time we hit the snow, while sliding sideways, we are at a full run. When the sled hits the snow, we are on the abrupt edge of the road itself. I get knocked off the runners and I am having flashbacks of my knee blow-out. Tying to run, my feet are hitting the ground about every 10 feet. During one of these monster strides, I look down and see where Steve's footprint hit the edge of the pavement where he broke his ankle. Instantly the sled straightens out as it hits the snow covered trail. I jump! I have one shot at landing on the runners. I land on them with both feet, the only problem is that one runner is in the snow and the other is about a foot in the air. I shift my weight and slam the airborne runner down onto the trail. We made it! My heart is pounding out of control. Easy now, easy you guys. That was close. I hope the mushers behind us make it through there smoother than we did.

The trail is getting better and the temperature is starting to drop. It's time for me to focus on the dogs. Do I see any abnormalities? The dogs are happy and are setting a nice pace. It isn't a race winning pace, but we aren't making mistakes and we aren't wasting any time. All the tug lines are tight. We are working as a team. The dogs are making small sounds to each other as they sniff and explore the new trail.

I don't see anymore mushers coming up from behind, so I figure that our pace must be competitive. We start the mild decent to the flats and approach the area I mentioned at the mushers' meeting, the half mile of moguls just prior to the hard downhill switchback to the left. The last time we went around this corner was in the 2005 race. I launched the sled into the air after we dead-centered a two foot snowball the big trail groomer left behind. I have more than once relived that crash in my head and have to admit it still spooks me. The moguls are straight ahead. As we bound over the rough trail, the dogs are being really manageable. No one is goofing off. Here comes the switchback. Easy kids. Easy now. There's a narrow smooth chute through the corner and by golly we are headed right into it. We are in the groove as we slide around the corner like we've done it all our lives. With a deep sigh of relief, I realize, all that worrying was for naught. We work our way to the open flats and it is all clouded in. Too bad, because our visiting mushers will miss one of the great views of Mount Shasta that this trail has to offer.

Casper and Pudges, are wandering back and forth on the trail. "Straight ahead Casper, straight ahead Pudges" I command. They don't seem to be paying attention, for they continue weaving back and forth as they head up the trail. Then I see it... OH NO!

Casper:

Everything is settling into place, and the young'uns behind me are in tune with each other. We made it past that big open bare spot with Pat floundering around like a fish out of water on the edge of that road. He hung on to the sled and got through it. Now his voice is calm, but I tell through the lines that he is still very worried and tired. I don't think humans realize that we feel what they feel-it runs through the lines to us. It is a learned trait. My pals will to have the opportunity to experience it during this race.

Uh oh! Here comes the sharp turn where Pat crashed the sled last time we were here! I'd better steer him into that smooth line. I look back... Pat is all wide-eyed as he slides around the corner. All right... He made it. Finally, I feel him relax his grip on the handlebars and his legs on the runners. That corner woke him up. He goes through the whole team, congratulating each of us. Pudges and I get extra praise for doing so well, leading him safely around the sharp turn.

Pat's feeling pretty good and the team is happy. We are traveling at a nice speed when I see it. OH NO! Low lying clouds. "Can you guys feel the moisture in the air? It rained hard here, not long ago." "What does that mean?" asked Elizabeth. "It means the trail could get really tough up ahead. We could get into bad snow where we could be breaking through the crust and sink, either one foot or all at once. It's very trying." "What will we do Casper?" they all ask at once. 'We will slow down, tough it out and get through it. If you stumble or fall, keep your feet moving and the rest of us will pull you up. Keep your pads spread out, especially you bigger dogs, Preacher, Rupert, Tipper, you got that?" "We got it Casper," they answer.

Pudges and I work our way back and forth to see if we can figure out where the best part of the trail is. "Straight ahead", Pat yells. Oh great, he doesn't even know what's coming with the rained soaked trail. Well, he is going to figure it out when we start breaking through. The snow's starting to crack and crunch under my pads. It finally happens. I break through the punchy snow, up to my belly. Step back up, go a ways and a foot breaks through. "OH NO", I hear Pat groan as he gets on the drag mat to slow us down. We don't need any shoulder injuries! His happy mood suddenly turns serious but stays positive and reassuring. The young dogs are responding well. If one dog stumbles the others are giving the extra effort to keep the sled moving steady. Wow this is cool. These young kids are really stepping it up.

All of us hear it at once, except Pat. I swear he must be hard of hearing. Dogs are yapping up ahead. There they are. It's that team from up north. The driver has the leaders by their collar line and is turning them onto the trail that heads to the ski park checkpoint. He is falling in the waist deep snow. He finally gets them going and they head out. We head to the left, the trail that we raced on winters ago. Pat sounds a little upset as he yells "GEE," for us to go right. Pat, it is to the left. "GEE Casper", he says, as he is coming toward us in snow up to his crotch. OK, OK, as Pudges and I swing the team to the right turn trail. Of course, Pat gets drug over by the lines but he manages to get back on his feet, grab the handlebar and jump back on the runners. Oh good, he's with us. I hear him huffing and puffing, trying to catch his breath. "OK, let's go to work", Pat shouts. Good! He's not upset. How was I supposed to know we were going to go a different way? Pat continues his praises, so all is well.

Pat:

Damn! Our firm trail has turned into punchy snow. I'd better slow them down or we'll pick up shoulder and wrist injuries. "I hope the big dogs take it easy," I tell myself. "Had I known this would happen I would have run a couple of smaller dogs instead of all our power dogs. Oh well, just deal with it, Pat. Just take your time and maybe, just maybe, we'll be all right."

In an instant the dogs become excited and try to take off. "Easy, easy you guys," I plead. We round a corner and I see what has them so worked up. Bino, from Oregon, is steering his team up the sharp trail back to the right, in soft deep snow. He has the leader's lines and is telling me this is his third try. Bino patiently works his dogs onto the trail. "GEE Casper", Casper heads to the left instead of right. "GEE, GEE, Casper", he's not listening. I set the snow hooks deep in the soft snow and run up to swing them to the right trail where Bino's team just headed. Casper finally understands and swings the team just as I fall face down in the snow. The snow hooks pop loose and the lines catch me about chest high. Somehow I manage to scramble up, grab the handlebar, and swing my feet onto the runners. The only other option was being left behind. Whew! I catch my breath while studying Bino's team as they ever so slowly pull away. He is running with smaller dogs than us and they are hardly breaking through the snow crust. That alone can make the difference in the speed, allowing him to pull away. It is discouraging to watch. I can't help the team because my foot sinks knee deep into the snow and jerks on the sled as I pull back onto the runners. It is just messing up their rhythm. All I can do is stand still and tell the kids how great they are doing. They are working well together. I like what I am seeing. There is determination in this team. I am feeling pretty good and let the team know it. We may pull this race off yet.

Casper:

Hey you guys! Recognize that smell? I bet once we get around this corner… Yep! Yipee! I know this place! Remember that sign? We ran this trail a moon cycle ago. It leads to the trailhead where Pat gives rides to the humans. It always makes me laugh when I see the looks on their faces as we head out around the first corner. They give us lots of loving, and the meat candy after every trip is tasty.

I'd better quit daydreaming and pay attention! The snow is down to where our paws are going all the way to the road underneath. The team wants to go faster because we don't have to deal with the deep, punchy snow. Hmm. Pat's voice is still lined with concern. The team is doing great so it must be the snow conditions that he has on his mind.

Pat:

The light of day is turning into a dark moonless night. All you can make out is the silhouettes of the trees and the dirt bank beside us. The rest is the fading whiteness of the snow. What I am to see next, I can't believe. Everything up ahead has turned dark black. Where is the snow? My God, it's gone! I was here two days ago marking the race trail and there was four to six inches of hard packed snow, with only an occasional small open patch. It must have just poured rain here!

The team looks back. I give the "Straight Ahead" command as they dash onto the dirt road surface. I run along the sled as long as I can and then hop on the runners. Just as my weight slows them down almost to a stop, I jump back off and run again until I'm winded. I'm tiring fast, but I'm still doing well for being almost 56 years old.

Suddenly the team looks back as the flash of a headlight hits us from behind. My competitive streak kicks in and we take off running again. The team is still gaining on us, so I stop to let them pass. Chris is jogging alone like it's no big deal! I, on the other hand, am huffing and puffing to catch my breath. I tell him how nice it must be to have fresh young legs. He just smiles with that look of respect that distance mushers share while out on the trail. I question myself about being out here competing with these much younger mushers, when the sled slams into a rock that has rolled down onto the trail. I look down with the headlamp and see that there are fist size rocks all over the trail. If I don't watch it, I will be the next casualty of the trail.

These terrible conditions seemed to continue forever, even though it may have only been half a mile, I don't know, but this snowless trail is really getting me down. All this hard work by so many good people and sponsors, and an unseasonable rain takes the last of our snow. What next?

Finally! Snow up ahead. Back on the runners again, I slump over the handlebars, try to catch my breath and grab a drink. The dogs seem surprisingly upbeat, taking off in a run uphill. They seem to know that our turnaround loop for the guided sled dog rides is just around the next corner. There is enough snow, so I to set the snowhooks to hold the team in place, and give everyone a nice salmon meat snack. They need the moisture and feeding fish is a good way to keep them hydrated. Everyone eats well and tails are wagging. I pull the snow hooks and off we go. This is more like it...

Casper:

Oh Boy. I smell lots of dirt coming. Pat's not going to like this. After that last bare spot fiasco, I wonder which side he'll want us on this time? Yep, there is the dirt. Well, I guess I don't have to worry about what side of the trail to run on. The whole darn trail is dirt. Wow. We've never run over rocks like this with the sled. I hear Tipper give out a grunt of pain. "Are you OK Tipper?" "Yip! I'll be alright. I just tripped on one of the rocks" says Tipper. "Hey everybody, focus on your footing or we are going to pick up a bunch of wrist injuries", "OK," they reply. This is half crazy.

Pat seems quiet and concerned. I know he and Lisa have a lot to do with organizing this race. Wish I could tell him it's not his fault that it rained. I sense that he's just about tuckered out. Come on Pat, hang in there. It's going to get better. It's cooling off. There must be snow up ahead where our loop turnaround is for the human rides. Ya, there's the snow. Pat jumps back onto the runners, trying to catch his breath. Soon he's digging into the sled bag. I look back and see him gulping down a drink. Good, he needs to keep hydrated. Next, I hear that wonderful sound of a plastic bag. TREATS! All right! Fish! We all get our share and things are looking up again. We head out in a dash and Pat is pleased.

"Hey Casper", Pat shouts. I look back. "You're a good boy. Thank you, Casper." I whirl my tail in thanks as my chest and eyes well-up with pride. "Come on kids. Follow me." "We're with you Casper," they yip back with puppy excitement.

Pat:

About 3 miles out from the first checkpoint, I see the first team approaching us. It's Katie from Montana and her Iditarod team. I call out "GEE" to the leaders and they swing over to the right side as Katie's team goes by on the left in a head-on pass. All I say to her was that there was snow on this trail two days ago. Her team looks sharp. They looked as though it is just business as usual. Teams that have been to the Iditarod have a certain air of confidence about them. Unless she screws up, the race is hers to win. Another mile or two and here comes Trent from Idaho running a puppy team from a kennel out of Michigan. His job is to give the pups the training miles they need to go to the Iditarod later in the season. They may then have the experience to run on the "A" team with their owner at the Iditarod the following year.

We run over more open spots of pavement. At least there is a strip of snow on the left and Casper does a nice job of keeping us on it. We pull into the checkpoint and Race Marshal, Bill, is there to check us in. I turn the team around and have them facing back out the trail. I can tell they are confused, because we normally come in from tours and go straight to the pickup where they are done for the day or have a long rest before they go back out. I quickly snack and water the dogs. My socks are soaked in sweat from running, so I sit down on the sled to change them when Bill approaches and asks, "Is it a good time to talk?" "You bet," I answer. He tells me of his concern about running us back over that section of dirt trail, a day from now. Since none of the mushers are actually using the race to qualify for the Iditarod, we could throw out that section of trail for the return trip without hurting any team's goals. It would shorten the race to 184 miles, from 220 miles. We decide that because the rain has made the trail conditions so tough that for the safety of the dogs and mushers we won't run over it, except to get back to the main trail. The decision is announced to the remaining mushers at the checkpoint, and you can see everyone's mood perk up.

Bino comes over and asks me if I have an extra light with me. His headlamp wiring isn't working and his spare is at the next checkpoint. He tried to fix it but didn't have the right tools. I give him my backup light that throws a poor narrow beam. He is happy to get anything! There is no moon and it is pitch black. Without a light he would have to just sit there until daylight with no chance to catch the rest of us by race's end. I am glad to help. It's just the right thing to do. We all like to move up in the race standings, but not this way. Now, I am a little concerned because my headlamp also has a tendency to go out at times. I press the wiring together and it usually works fine. I do have another small headlight along as a back up.

Bino heads out of the checkpoint looking strong, Chris follows shortly in pursuit. Their smaller dogs look friskier than my team of larger dogs. Don't worry about it Pat, they only had 20 dogs to train… we trained 60 for the guide business. My kids are all jumping and lunging as the other teams head out. I guess I don't have to worry about them not wanting to leave. I make sure that they all get plenty of meat snacks and water, sign out, pull the snow hook and give the command, "Team Hup!" We're off in a dash. Thirty eight miles down, one hundred and forty six miles left to finish!

Casper:

Hey guys, look! There's a light up ahead! It must be a team coming towards us, "Let's look sharp!" Pat gives the, "GEE, ON BY," command so Pudges and I swing the team to the right and complete a perfect head on pass. Pat says something to the other dog driver, but I hear nothing in return. I feel Pat's concerns but he tells us, "It's OK." That team and driver are dialed in. I heard that they have run the Iditarod, whatever that is. They look fast. Some of the kids mention how fast they are. "Can we catch them Casper?" some ask. I tell them sternly, "We need to run our race. Don't worry about them. Our job is to finish and that is all we have to think about."

Soon another team approaches with tails wagging. We pass and exchange a few niceties. They have a lot of young dogs too! That sure perks the kids up! As we approach the Ski Park Trailhead I see more open dirt spots on the trail. After that last ordeal…This time I wait for Pat's command, "Casper HAW". Pudges and I lead the team to the left onto a narrow path of snow. I get an Atta-Boy from Pat and we head to the trailhead.

Where's the pickup? Pat turns us around to face the trail we came in on, then waters and snacks us. I guess this isn't the end of the race yet! Pat takes break, changes his socks, and has a short talk with some guy. Whatever they discussed, Pat seems happier. He then gives a headlight to some guy called Bino. Soon they head out onto the trail. I try to jerk the snow hook loose, but to no avail. Pat tells me to, "Settle down." He collects the water pans, and repacks the sled. Then…we are off again. Heck, this is good fun.

THE TEAM

To the Pilgrim Creek Checkpoint and Mandatory Rest

Pat:

As we head back over the bare spots to the snowmobile park trail system, they don't seem as vast traveling downhill. As we meet the last team in the race, I give some encouraging words. When we get back to the intersection where we had trouble before, Casper looks back. "GEE Casper". "Yeah, Yeah," I tell him, as he gives me the, I knew it was this way, look. He has that big smile on his face.

Casper:

After we go through the spot where we knocked Pat over in the snow with the lines, I look back and tease Pat with my, I told you so look. Not much later, I feel someone out of sync. Looking back and I see that it is Tipper. I bark, "How are you doing?" Tipper says, "My left front wrist is getting sore." "Hang in there and Pat will treat it at the next trailhead. It's only about five miles ahead!

I smell smoke and some really good cooking. "Hey you guys, there's a big rest area just up ahead!" The team speeds up. It couldn't have come at a better time. The young pups are starting to get tired.

As we approach the turn leading us into the rest area, I am confused by the little lights hanging all over the trees. On the right, there is a tent with a big fire nearby. I finally realize Pat is yelling

HAW. I swing us to the left into the woods. I couldn't hear him with all the people talking and the team between us barking in excitement. The lights are on both sides of us now and humans are there to lead us to our rest spot. They turn us around so we are pointed in the right direction when we are ready to leave. Pat walks over to a pile of stuff and brings back a big bag full of wood shavings and puts some down for each of us. Pat looks exhausted, but continues to tend to the chores. Hardly able to pick up his feet, he still takes care of us before himself. Lord knows I love that man. He takes off our booties and heads to Tipper. Soon Pat is massaging his sore wrist with that warming goo. The last I hear is Tipper moaning in pleasure and appreciation, as I doze off into a deep sleep.

Pat:

Wow, we made it! There are the lights at the Pilgrim Creek Trailhead. There's lots of work to do here. I need to utilize all my moves so I can save time and energy both for the dogs and myself. Right now, I am feeling out of practice. If I can get them to settle into a rest cycle soon, it will pay off later in the race.

Once again, like at the start of the race, my mind is shifting through the work I have to do. It is overwhelming. I have to focus and get it together. Get the dogs on the wood shavings. Off with their booties. Check and apply the Algyval ointment to their feet and wrists. Replace the sled's runner covers. The list in my head keeps growing.

We approach the left turn into the wooded area where we will rest for at least the four hour mandatory period, and possibly longer. What a sight. Mary and her volunteers, many whom work with her at the USFS, have outdone themselves. Tents. Bonfires. Glow sticks. It looks like an airport runway as we approach! At the turn pointing into the woods the trail of lights and volunteers, lead the way. I call out "HAW" to Casper, but he is oblivious. All the people pointing, the campfire, and glow sticks must have him confused. I laugh, as I picture him thinking he is in a time warp, back to the late 60's! I yell "HAW' again and again, until Casper finally looks back at me. I yell HAW one more time. He snaps out of it and takes off in a dash to the left onto the trail. I can tell that the dogs are amazed at the lights lining the way. They pull to the right, which puts the sled down into a hole, big enough swallow a truck. The volunteers are hollering, "Do you need help?" I let out a whoop as we pop out over the other side. They must think I'm crazy… I like to think so! We wind our way through the big timber, past the other teams already in, tie off the sled, and swing the team around facing the direction we will be taking off.

It's time to go to work. I head over to the pile of supplies underneath a suspended tarp, grab the bag of wood shavings, and put some down for each dog. Each dog gets a snack on my way up the team. The booties come off the dogs' feet on the way back. The Algyval ointment has been kept warm in my coat pocket. I start to apply it to the dog's feet and wrists, starting with Tipper, who was showing a slight limp about five miles back. He moans and groans with pleasure as I massage the swelling back up into his leg and put a wrist wrap on the sore area. When I fold the wrist in and squeeze, he doesn't whimper with pain. He will be able to continue after a good rest. Tipper seems to be the only dog with a problem. The important word here is "seems."

Next the dogs are offered kibble and water. Some partake. Some are already resting. There are 4 dogs still sitting or standing. After some petting and soft words I get two of them to lie down. Snowy and her daughter Lady are still standing. I decide not to worry about it and go about my business. Everything is coming very slowly for me. I can't seem to find anything that I had packed just hours before.

Dr. Erica approaches and asks if there are any issues with my dogs. No, "Just myself Erica, I can't seem to find anything!" I show her Tipper's wrist and the treatment given to him, she seems pleased but, still concerned. After a pause, she finally says what she has on her mind. "When do you plan to get some sleep Pat?" I must really look like hell for her to say that. I tell her probably not until we get to the Four Corners Checkpoint. There's more to do here. I still have to change the sled's runner covers. That doesn't work for her, so I tell her I will close my eyes as soon as I can. She smiles and tells me to find her if I need a dog looked at and informs me about the great food at the warming hut. I decline, because leaving all these young dogs alone doesn't seem to smart. I haven't had a chance to camp with them yet. I don't know how they will behave and I have plenty of food packed with us. I thank her as she heads to the warming hut.

The last hammering sounds of someone changing their runner covers, remind me of my next task. Setting my gloves down, I get out the tools and spare set of runner covers. When laying the sled over on its side my heart skips a beat. The left runner cover has separated from the runner with a three inch gap. The separation is where the runners curve up in the front of the sled. There doesn't seem to be any damage to the dovetail guide that the runner cover slides onto, although there is a lot of mud and sand packed in, along with frozen snow and ice. Well, let's do it. First, I unscrew the front bolt that runs through the whole runner and runner cover, then, pry the screwdriver under the runner cover to get it started. I grab hold and peel the cover off the runner. Next, I closely inspect the dovetail guide and try my best to clean the sandy grit along the guide with my pocketknife. The cover slides on, but it's getting tougher and tougher to gain on it. It's on about halfway when it comes to a stop. A couple of cuss words slip past my lips and I hope no has heard me. I'm so tired and frustrated. Blah, Blah, Blah. Nobody put you here but you, so quit feeling sorry for yourself. I decide to take a break, have a sandwich, a power drink and rethink the situation. I need something to lubricate the runner. After relaxing, I come up with the idea to back the cover off and apply some of the salve that I use on the dog's wrists. I smear it on the whole length of the runner and try again. Hey, it's working! The last foot of the runner moves on at about a quarter inch at a time with the aid of my ax hitting the screwdriver in the bolt hole, but by golly we got it. The other runner cover goes on a lot easier than the first and I am pretty proud of myself. In past years I probably would have had a fit, which would make the job a whole lot harder. The worst part is that it would make the dogs nervous. Snowy and Lady are sitting now, so I decide to lie down in the sled and get some rest.

My mind drifts to the dogs that are lined out ahead of me.

Casper.....my buddy. A seven year old male, cream colored with a reddish back and head. I almost lost him last September to a misdiagnosed lower intestinal blockage. I finally took him to another hospital and told them to have the operating table ready or I could loose him within hours. They had him open on the operating table and removed seven inches of lower intestine due to blockage! Casper and I had always been close, but this developed our bond and appreciation for each other like never before. I savor every moment of following behind him. He has been such a kind and noble friend.

Pudges.....a five year old hybrid, Husky/German shorthair cross. I gave her away as a pup because she had such short legs and body. When they moved away I got Pudges back. When I went to fight fires for a month, came home and barely recognized her. She stretched and slimmed out into a body of an athlete. A very smart, calm and trouble free dog that fits well beside Casper's high intensity. She ran this course as a yearling and toughed it out with a bruised foot.

Cheena.....and Panda.....run the point positions behind Casper and Pudges. Sisters of the same litter, just over two years of age. Cheerleaders running their rookie race. I'm looking forward to spring training, because I think they will both make leaders. They have a thicker coat so I must keep an eye on them when the weather warms.

Snowy.....seven years old. The last time she was here I should have taken her out of the race. She simply wasn't feeling well. On top of it, she got so amped up that it zapped her energy and I ended up packing her in the sled from ten miles out, with another forty five to go. Hopefully, that won't happen again this race. A very quiet dog, unlike her vocal brother, Casper.

Lady.....Snowy's daughter, four years old. It's her first distance race. She is quiet like her mother... A trouble free, steady girl. They compliment each other and I rarely have to say a word to either of them.

Patchy.....a female only a year and a half old. Super dog. I have never had to teach or say anything to her from day one. Very calm, attentive and smart. She has been running in lead for the guide business. A real diamond in the rough. She has identical sisters that I believe will follow in her footsteps. A real pleasure to work with. We look forward to many miles together.

Sheenje.....a very special two year old, all white female leader. She is named after one of my best dog friends, who passed on after eighteen wonderful years. The name Sheenje means spirit dog in Apache. As a two month old pup she broke her main front right leg bone while running through the river rocks. I picked her up and put a wrist wrap on it. She stayed still for weeks until it healed and she has never looked back. I didn't think I would ever be able to use her but she had other ideas. This is her rookie race as well as her partner beside her, Patchy. Her work ethic, friendly and lovable attitude has worked herself into a spot on the team. She is not super fast because of her short length, but don't tell her that. She does more than her share and keeps a nice pace when put in the lead. A special little girl.

Rupert.....a lovable floppy eared, brown, black and white four year old male. I never know what he is thinking. He never seems excited about anything, except other girl dogs. He can run lead but has never felt comfortable there. We used to give rides on a trail where sometimes we would turn back early. He would get to that spot and try to turn us around. When things get confusing or tough he has the habit of wanting to turn around. This is his rookie race, so I really don't know what to expect if he gets tired. He has all the natural physical skills and works very hard, but I always worry about what is going on between his ears.

Preacher.....a four year old female that looks a lot like Rupert with the same long, smooth, strong stride. She also runs lead and has a great work ethic. She is a bit shy but runs with confidence and is always there when you ask for a little bit more. It is also her rookie race. My only concern is that she has a sensitive stomach at times so I have to watch how she is eating and drinking. So far all looks well.

Tipper.....a big, all black, long, sleek beautiful two year old male at his rookie race. I bred him with Panda earlier this year for the future of the kennel. A smooth trotter and graceful when loping. He is having a tough time of it in this punchy snow. I am concerned about his wrists although I have seen worse ankles than his go on to finish without problems in past races. That was on a solid good trail, unlike what we are dealing with today. I hope the trail firms up tonight. That will help him finish the race. With my own size and weight of over 225 pounds, I need all the dog power that I can muster! Boy, I hope we don't have to pack him in the sled!

Elizabeth......a long, slim, ivory blonde rookie female, nearing two years of age. She is the fastest dog on the team, so why do I have her in wheel position in front of the sled? She runs great in lead, but she has a tendency to wear the team out by running them too fast. If we are close to moving up a position during the race, then I will put her up in lead.

I pop my headlamp on and see that Snowy and Lady have finally laid down to rest. Good maybe I can catch a few zzzzz's.

The next leg of the race is going to show what this team is really made of. It's a tough climb that starts only a few miles out and the snow is still punchy. Are these kids as tough as I think they are?

I'm often asked why mushers put themselves and their dogs into the conditions and challenges these races throw at you. Challenge is a key word. I crave the challenge and believe the dogs do too. What is the fun of doing something you know is going to be easy? The fun is in working through situations where you don't have control of all the factors. That's when the pride and satisfaction of accomplishment takes over, of not only in yourself, but also in your dogs.

The yipping and yapping of Katie's team wakes us up. She's preparing her team to head out. Her dogs have gotten some extra rest over the mandatory four hours. Good move Katie. The more rest, the faster the average speed on the trail. I know Bino wants to stay with her so he will leave and loose the extra rest time. By the last leg of the race, that may be a huge advantage for Katie and her team.

Most of my dogs are resting and paying no attention except Casper. Nothing gets by Casper. I swear he not only observes. He analyses and problem solves too!

My hands have started to chill. Where are my favorite gloves? They are nowhere to be found. Not in my coat or my pants. I end up going through the whole sled. Nowhere! I head over to the cache of supplies and they aren't there either. Again I search through my pockets, the sled and back to the drop bags. There are only so many places they can be. What the hell. They just can't walk off on their own. I go back through everything once again. Nothing! By now I am just plain pissed off. If this is one of those tests, I have just badly failed. I give up! I have another pair of leather gloves as a backup, but if they get wet, I will be up this punchy trail without a paddle.

To warm my hands and cool my temper, I head over to the bonfire. I don't want the dogs to be effected by my irritated state. Mary comes over and must have seen that I wasn't myself. I tell her that I am so mentally fried that I can't do simple tasks. She gives me a needed hug and tells me to hang in there. Sometimes that is all we need. She heads back to the warming cabin as I sit down, beside the fire, under the canopy of stars. While looking into the flames, I realize they have calmed my spirit. I wonder if I even thanked Mary. I owe her one.

Katie heads out with Bino soon in chase. Chris is preparing to leave. Casper and a few of the other dogs are up and looking at me. Casper looks confident but the rest of the team has an almost a sad, scared look. They have probably picked up on my mood, so I will have some cheerleading to do.

Casper:

I'm awakened by the wonderful sounds of dogs ready to go. Pat is looking all over for something. It would be so much easier if he'd just use that big nose of his to find whatever it is he is looking for. I just don't understand humans sometimes.

In all the years we have traveled together, I have never seen Pat so tired. I am concerned. He is usually happy and upbeat. Our eyes meet, and I give him my, "I'm ready to go look". He smiles and says, "You are something else Casper." We share a little chuckle, as he tells me that we are going to rest a bit longer. He walks over to the fire nearby and seems to be drifting off into the soothing flames. He doesn't seem to realize that I have his back and the best of this team is yet to come. "Get some rest my good friend."

As I lie back down, I let the other dogs know to settle down too. Hang in there Pat.

Pat:

A popping noise from the fire jolts me out of a half lucid dream. Back to reality! We are in a dog race. Instantly, a quick check of my watch and I see it is about 2:40 am, a good time to start preparing to leave. We've taken a little over the mandatory four hour rest, which will work fine. As I approach the team, many of them stand up to greet me, and of course Casper is ready to go with tail a-wagging.

I remember the first distance race we entered years ago. It was the 350 mile, Race To The Sky, in Montana. I didn't know how to gauge when the dogs had rested enough. My good friend Jack, the race marshal, told me when the first dog on your team wakes on its own, gets up and has a good stretch, then most likely the rest of the team is ready to go. The team actually is acting a bit antsy. I pull out the bag of treats, and each dog gets its share of tripe, sausage and fish. They ate their kibble and drank earlier so they are all looking pretty good. Since the trail hasn't frozen up any more, I decide to bootie just a few of the dog's pads that need more protection. I give one last massage to Tipper and apply the warming salve to all the dog's pads and ankles. Tipper is still sore, but when I walk him, he only shows a slight limp. I decide to keep him in the race. If I am wrong, then we may have to pack him. This could drop us way back in speed and standings. If the trail has firmed up, I believe he will be all right. There's always lots of, "Ifs."

I pack the checkpoint supplies and place them under the tarp for the return trip. Judy, checks out our mandatory gear supplies that must go with us in the sled. The team, already knowing the way, easily maneuvers us through the big timber and back onto the main trail. We head out and everyone seems happy. The trail is in fact firmer, due to the groomed trail and the cooler weather. Tipper's wrist is loosening up as we go. The trail up to 4 Corners Checkpoint should be groomed the whole way, with plenty of snowpack. Its 3:30 am, we're 61 miles into the race, have taken over a 4 hour break and the team is traveling well. We lost three weeks of training earlier in the season, due to repairs on both the septic line and a cracked water tank at the cabin. Because of that, we didn't have the opportunity to train a forty mile run, nor did we have the time to do any back-to-back runs after a rest cycle. Needless to say, I am pleased, giving the dogs praise, and calling out each dog by name. I think of my fiancée, Lisa. I send her a mental message that we are all fine and that I love her. OK Guys, let's keep up the good work! Little do we know what is next in store for us next!

LAUGH IT UP

To Four Corners Checkpoint

Casper:

A slow crunch, crunch on the snow. Pat's working his way back from the fire. I stand at attention, swirling my tail. He picks up on my readiness and starts to work on all our feet and wrists again. Ohhhh, that feels good. Tipper's wrist gets some extra attention and Pat gives him a walk around on his leash. He's doing his best to hide the soreness so Pat won't take him out of the race. Some of the other kids have also been complaining of sore wrists. My front wrist is a bit stiff too! That has never happened to me before. I'm concerned but don't let anyone know, for fear that it may affect the confidence of the team, or even worse, Pat. The punchy trail sure took its toll.

Ahhh…the glorious sound of the sled zipper followed by the meat pouches being cut open means none other than...treat time. Wow! Belly fat. Fish. Sausage. And lots of it! We're all worked up as we plea our personal request for more. Our aches and sore spots are forgotten as we lunge against our harnesses to reach the treats. Pat is worked up too! This excitement builds at every hook up. It's something we will always share. At times, I believe Pat and I are even sharing the same thoughts.

Pat calls out the familiar, "OK Hup" and we confidently pull back onto the main trail. After the first couple of miles, we loosen into a nice pace. As the trail slowly begins to climb, I feel the smooth trail is still soft. We are barely able to stay on top without breaking through. I try not to show my concern. The others are quiet, and are aware of the precarious snow too. Pat's back there trying to help by peddling up the hill but he is breaking through and disrupting our rhythm. I want to tell him to steer. We will take care of the rest. This side hill is hard on Tipper's bad wrist, as well as the rest of the team, but there is no complaining. We're really focused, and although we aren't going very fast, there is no lack of effort. These kids are growing up before my eyes. The strong feelings bring tears to my eyes, when I realize I have to hold my feelings firm, at least until the race is over.

Climb and climb. This is a tough hill. As we come around a corner our nice smooth trail turns rough again. It looks like a scrambled mess. Whatever did this, left a trail of rough cross ridges on the outside with just some smooth parts in the middle. To make matters worst, the snow is getting punchy again and we're breaking through. This will probably do-in Tipper's wrist. He is showing a noticeable limp. His head is bobbing as he powers up hill with his three good legs, giving it all he has. What a shame. His determination makes me proud to be a sled dog. I go to encourage Tipper but Pat beats me to it. The team responds to Tipper's effort and all pitch in. The speed increases until Pat gently applies the brake. I give Pat a stern look to say, "What the heck are you doing?" He replies, "Tipper can't keep up at that speed and if we don't back off, we'll have to pack him in the sled." I understand and send the message to ease off a bit to the others. I make eye contact with

Tipper and give him the "job well done" sign. He is embarrassed but appreciates the praise.

The long climb continues. Finally, the rough trail clears up and the snow has firmed to where we are able to stay on top of it again. Pat is doing a nice job of encouraging us up the steep grade and he is running and helping out whenever he can. The tougher things get, the more determination he projects! I don't know where he gets it from but it sure is motivating these young pups!

The top if the ridge is just ahead and we all know it. A sense of accomplishment runs through the team. Pat brings us to a stop and we all get a nice treat and lots of atta-boys. He talks gently to Tipper, telling him how good he is doing, picks him up and places him in the sled. Tipper doesn't want to ride and tries to jump out. I see Pat hook a line from each side of the sled to his collar to keep Tipper in place.

I got dehydrated in my first race in Big Sky Country and Pat had to pack me in the sled. All the bouncing and noise scared the heck out of me. I tell Tipper, "It's OK, Pat's packing you for your own good." Tipper nods and reluctantly settles into the bag while accepting Pat's gentle strokes. Now, we have to head down the steep grade on the other side. Pat whispers to me, "Casper, we need to take it easy." Boy, that's going to be hard to do with these young'uns chomping at the bit to take this downhill run. To say the least, this is going to be interesting.

Pat:

The team is doing wonderfully! We are well into the long climb over Fons Butte. Tipper still shows a slight limp but it doesn't seem to be getting worse. Something is starting to happen within this team. They are working as a unit... Sure we had a lot of good training runs, but this is different, like they have a goal to attain. This is a change of attitude.

While contemplating this progressive attitude, out of nowhere the whole team is out of sync. The snow grooming machine has messed up the trail. It was like they quit dragging the grooming part that does the grooming and just rode the unit up the trail. To make matters worst, because it hadn't packed the trail, the dogs are breaking through the snow again. For a brief period, I am cussing the groomer until I finally deduct that there must have been a malfunction. Amazingly, it really doesn't get under my skin. It's just another obstacle to overcome. The dogs don't seem too distressed by it either. They just continue. Business as usual. I'm really encouraging the dogs on how well they are doing, especially Tipper. Unfortunately, I can see that I won't be able to let Tipper run down the other side on his bad wrist. I am so proud of the effort and guts that he is showing. I wish I had taken him out of the race back at Pilgrim Creek, but had I done that, I would never have seen his character and work ethic. He has a bright future ahead. Next, I move Rupert into wheel with Elizabeth in Tipper's spot.

I've only run this section of trail once before, many years ago. Casper may have been with us. It was the winter that I started dating Lisa. We went out after dark on a full moon, and what a fun run that was. The part that is a challenge to navigate is on the other side of this hill where I will have to pack Tipper in the sled. We get to the top, I snack everyone and try to calm Tipper, for what is next to come.

With a soft reassuring voice, I place him in the sled. The wrestling match begins. He wants no part of riding. I give him a couple of persuasive taps on his nose. He half sits in the sled. I pull the snow hook and we are off. Tipper instantly tries to lunge out of the sled, I grab his collar. I have to drop the snow hook to secure a grip on the handle bar. While applying the brake the snow hook is flying and bouncing alongside my ankle on the runner, I have to loop my left arm around the handle bar and onto Tipper's collar. Next with the dogs at a full gait, I reach down for the flying snow hook and somehow manage to get it in position and regain control. The next three to four miles seemed to last forever. When we hit the flat at the valley floor, Tipper finally relaxes in the sled and we settle back into a nice pace. The dogs are pleased with themselves while my upper body is worn out.

I notice that Elizabeth is not pulling very hard which is very unusual. She doesn't seem injured, but she is definitely not her happy self. She is my little cheerleader, I need to keep a close eye on her.

I am surprised at how well we are moving with Tipper in the sled. It dawns on me then... why not? We regularly have 600 lbs. on the sled when we give guided rides. As we pass through an intersection, I can tell the dogs recognize this part of the trail from two years ago with the ATV. Sled dogs have amazing memories. They remember trails from years ago. Even if you were there in the summer on dirt, they will be able to follow it on sixty inches of snow. How they do it, I have no idea.

I can't keep my attention off Elizabeth so I stop to give the dogs a short rest and I give her a good look over. Her feet look good. She has one slightly sore wrist, and her shoulders are fine. When pulling her hide up off her neck, it doesn't snap back into position fast enough. Upon checking her gums it appears as though she could have some dehydration. We don't have, water with us so I dig through the snacks and come up with some fish. Fish is over 90 % water, she gets as much as she wants. Hopefully that does the trick.

It's almost daylight. The rising sun awakens the team one dog at a time. Tipper is not happy in the sled, Elizabeth isn't pulling, but she is keeping up with the rest. Lady is taking it easy on a wrist when going down hill, but all-in-all, their attitudes are good.

I closely watch Elizabeth travel. She squats to pee and instead of a light golden color, it is turning towards a light brown color. This is bad news. It is a sign that the dog has run out of stored water and is drawing moisture from muscle tissue. We are about twelve miles from the Four Corners checkpoint. We really don't want to have to pack Elizabeth in the sled with Tipper so I ask Casper to "take it easy" once again. I don't have to explain to him why, this time. All of the injuries are starting to add up. The team has turned very quiet and serious. I hope I am not losing them. I've never had a team shut down on me but I have passed teams that have shutdown.

I decide it's time to lighten the mood. I start singing some light, happy, Irish tunes, while mixing in the names of all the dogs in the team. Their mood perks up. They seem to enjoy the silly tunes mixed in with whistling, barks, grunts, belches and flatulent sounds. Of course, I blame Casper and tell him his butt stinks... to the delight of the other dogs. We are having fun. Pretty soon, we are at the top of the rise, ready to drop down into Four Corners Checkpoint. Most of the team has trained on this stretch and know exactly how far it is to the trailhead.

It's a good time to snack them. Tipper wants out. I let him out to pee and potty, tell him he's special, and put him back in. Before we head down the hill, I give every dog lots of loving. Lady is limping a little, Elizabeth is hanging in there. I was concerned that she would give up, but like Tipper she is giving it her all. No matter how fast the team wants to run into the checkpoint, I must keep them slowed down due to Lady's wrist and, Elizabeth still looks weak. They are anxious, so I pull the snow hook and begin singing a calming song. Even though we are beat up, we are happy and still traveling. "You guys are awesome".

This is the first moment that I believe we are going to finish, no matter what this race throws at us. We're banged up, but we are mentally strong. I have my second wind. Everyone is looking forward to some great food, and a nice nap. Snow is coming by midday.

Casper:

Pat yanks the snow hook and we're off. I'm doing my best to keep a gentle pace but it's no use. Pudges, China, Panda, Snowy, Patchy, Sheenje, Rupert and Preacher are powering down the hill through its sweeping turns. I look back at Pat. He's floundering around again. Looks like Tipper is being a handful. Pat grasps for the flying snow hook, (love the man), but he really is too tall for this sport. He finally gains control… Or should I say, as controlled as Pat gets. He would do a lot better if he were smaller. I remember at a race up north, he was standing alongside a tiny little woman named Wendy. She fit underneath Pat's armpit! Sure would be fun to pull a sled with someone that light on the runners. No offence, Pat.

We hit the flats and everything is going fine, when, I hear Pat yell, "whoa!" Next there's a big thud! I see Pat hit the snow on his side and is still holding Tipper. He's being dragged but somehow he manages to get the snow hook set. I'm slowing the team to a stop. As he gets up and dusts the snow off, he catches me looking at him and looks away in embarrassment. I don't know how he managed to tip over, but I bet he won't be telling anyone about that screw-up! With a timid "OK, Hup" from Pat, we head out again.

Elizabeth is complaining about feeling weak and thirsty. I ask if she has been drinking plenty of water. She tells me that with all the excitement, she may not have drunk at the vet check or at the first checkpoint. This is serious business…I explain that she is dehydrated and that the next time Pat snacks, she should eat all the fish she can. I tell her, "Take it easy Lizzy, you don't have to always try to outwork us." The other dogs chuckle and it uplifts Lizzy's spirit.

Along with the monotony of the continuous hills, I feel that the team moral is slowly slipping away. Lizzy isn't herself, and the other dogs are starting to complain and ask how long until the next rest spot. I encourage them by example as we march up and over the next rise. I am out of ideas on how to keep their spirits up, when out of the clear blue, Pat starts a wild and silly song that includes our names. I had no idea humans could make those sounds! Within minutes, all of us are in tears of laughter. My side is starting to hurt from laughing. Lord it feels good to laugh that hard. I can't remember the last time I had such a good laugh. Pat has always been loving, and kind… disciplinarian when necessary… but a clown? I will never look at him the same and we're a team again!

Within no time we are at the top of the ridge. Pat stops to snack and praise us. I have the time to think about what just happened. Just when I thought the team had hit bottom, Pat pulled the comedy act and took the whole bunch of us along for the ride. I am so proud of him! In the past, he had a tendency to get uptight when things go wrong. What a transformation, it was genius!

When we start out again everyone is pulling. Lizzy feels better. Tipper will be sitting out the rest of the race. Lizzy could continue, but it would be asking a lot, and Lady is hiding her sore wrist from Pat. Despite it all, when I looked back over the team, there was a sparkle in their eyes that I have never seen before. Something special is happening with the team and I know Pat feels it too.

Pat starts a slow soft song. It is beautiful! 'Reminds me of the wonderful morning and evening songs that he asks us to join him with. Standing on the balcony of the old log cabin, he starts with a soft AHOOOOOO, followed by OOOOWHAAWHAAWHAAOOOOOOOOOOOOO. The rest of us join the song and fill in the notes and ranges. My favorites are when we all stop at the same time and it turns instantly, eerily quiet. Then that Pat is as close to being one of us as any human can be. At that point, "The Bond" naturally begins. This is a good day, a good day, indeed.

I smell it! There is snow coming in. I wonder how much?

DOG CARE

Four Corners Checkpoint

Pat:

There's the checkpoint. The drop bags are lined up on the right. I check in with Paul, a volunteer. At about 8:40 AM., we swing the team to the right and I tie the quick release line from the sled to a tree. We are in the open, along side the trail, ready to head back out.

I take Tipper out of the sled and place him back in the team. Next I spread woodchips for each dog. They don't seem to notice me as they are already flat on their sides, falling into a deep sleep. I take off their booties and apply ointment to their feet and wrists and water Elizabeth, who enjoys the long needed drink. Soon, I am watering and feeding the rest of the team. It's good to see the dogs relaxed, laying out in the morning sunshine, getting their well deserved rest.

It is time to take Tipper on that long slow walk to inform Dr. Doug that I am scratching him from the team. After Dr. Doug finishes looking over Chris's team he marks Tipper out of the race. I hook a walker line to Tipper's collar as we head to his dog box on the pickup. Tipper wants no part of leaving the team and begins to put up a battle. He has a frantic look in his eyes. I kneel down beside him, give him a big hug, telling him that, "It's OK", and that I am proud of the great job he has done the team. Casper lets out a bark and I tell Casper, "It's OK, I'll take good care of him." We try it again. He catches a glimpse at the truck and quits resisting. As I lift him, he jumps up into his box. Tipper receives some more loving as I close the door to the box. I am feeling bad as I walk back to the team, wondering if there was some way, I could have prevented his injury… I never allowed them to run fast early in the race, I kept them at an easy pace through the punchy snow specifically to prevent wrist and shoulder injuries. Most wrist problems are from running too fast downhill on hard packed trails. This is another one of those experiences in the learning curve of distance racing. The team comes back into view and my mind turns my attention back to the matters at hand.

Dr. Doug and his tech students are looking over the team, they keep inspecting the dog's foot pads and I ask the tech students if they know what to look for in sore wrists. Soon, I am showing them the puffiness on the top of a dog's wrist joint and how to properly message the ointment in. We work our way through the whole team comparing a healthy wrist to a sore wrist. Lady has one sore and slightly stiff wrist, but doesn't whimper when it is tucked up and I apply pressure. Casper has a wrist that has slight swelling on top but he is paying no attention to it, so I am not too concerned. I'm afraid if I were to loose him, we wouldn't finish the race!

Across the road Katie and Chris are chatting. I hesitantly work my way over to them. Katie is in a good mood, (as would I if I were in her position). Her team looks great. They are having wrist problems too! Chris also had to pack a dog or two during that last section of trail. He is talking about scratching. Katie straightens him out of that thought process. His dogs notice that we are talking about them and his leaders stand up at attention. Soon the rest of his team is standing there with tension on their tug lines. I tell them I may have to drop another dog or two before we leave but have no thought of pulling out of the race! As I walk away I remember what Jack told me in Montana when I was losing confidence in my team the team. He told me, "Give them the chance." (We went on in that race to finish our first 350 miler). I stop, turn around and say, "Give them a chance Chris." I hope he heard me.

Here comes Trent and his team into the checkpoint, looking steady and in good condition. I help him get his team turned around into the trees behind me. He gets blankets out for his. They are a bunch of old blankets cut up, all of different colors. While I am walking away I have a private laugh thinking of out first race in Montana. We had to run the teams through a couple of thousand people. We put booties on all the dog's feet to protect them from the pavement. I had a friend make the booties out of scrap cloth from the polar fleece tops that she designed. All the booties were of different colors and print. I heard someone walk by and comment on them and her friend said, "What do you expect. That team is from California!"

It is time for me to catch some zzzz's, so I prop up against a tree, settle in and soon I'm asleep. Shortly I wake up by the sounds of Katie's team preparing to leave. As they head up onto the trail beside us, Casper and Pudges jump up and swing our team over onto the trail, ready to follow. I lead them back to their beds and help settle them down. This happens twice again as Bino and Chris leave with their teams. Lesson learned. Don't park your team where other teams are going to go by you! As Chris leaves, I yell to him, "They look good." We all have needed some encouragement in our first distance race. I just hope that when we head out, it is with the same intensity as his team.

I return to my napping spot and try to get in a little more rest. Snow is starting to fall and I think about the sprint races at the Deer Mountain Trailhead. I hope Lisa isn't stressing too bad over all the activity. Two years ago I was the Race Marshal and helped oversee the weekend activities. It can be overwhelming. I send her good thoughts and prayers of support. One of the Search and Rescue folks informs me that it's dumping snow at Deer Mountain. My thought process goes from worrying about the shortage of snow to dealing with too much snow. This country is known to easily dump a foot per hour!

A chill that has settled into my lower body awakens me. I see that it is starting to snow. The team is in deep sleep, so I head to the warming hut to change my socks, say "Hi" and thank our volunteers, vet and vet tech students. The layout of food, is a sight for sore eyes. I start with the soup and work my way from one end of the table to the other end. Nothing helps your attitude more during a distance race than some hot food and a little rest. I'm feeling good. As I head out the door, I inform the time keeper that within a half hour I need him to check my sled bag for mandatory gear so we can leave when we are ready.

As I approach the team, Casper is awake and seems to know it is time to leave. He humps his back up and reaches out into a long low stretch. One dog is up, so the rest of them should be ready. I get the snack bag out and as I break it open the smell of fresh meat has the whole team up on their feet, jumping all about. Elizabeth squats to pee and I closely watch for the color. It's back to natural, but she's still not herself. I check Lady over and walk her around. Although the swelling has gone away, and she seems to be in no pain, there's still a slight hitch in her step. Casper isn't paying any attention to his wrist and his sore spot has no swelling. I decide that even though Elizabeth seems once again hydrated, with her light frame it would be best to leave her behind. Her tail wags when I speak to her but she still is not herself. Even though she has replenished her tank, her tank is a lot smaller. She has done one hell of a job. Many dogs in her condition would have quit, but she worked through it. She, like Tipper, has shown what they are made of. Although I am saddened by having to pull her from the race, I don't let her know it. I lead her over to the truck. She gets nothing but praise. I let Tipper out for a break so Elizabeth can see that he is going to be staying with her. I place them in boxes side by side for moral support. They receive their last hugs and I inform the vet that I have withdrawn Elizabeth from the race.

When I get back to the team, Paul helps me take a section out of the lines to shorten and compact the team for more efficiency. The dogs are ready to go. As I have, they have seen enough of this place. The next leg of the race will tell the story. What will they do when we have to go back up that steep climb where we had Tipper in the sled? If we get over that, we'll finish. It will be all downhill back into Pilgrim Creek. If I have to walk the last 25 miles to the finish line, I'll do it….Boy I hope it doesn't come to that.

Casper:

"There's our next rest stop, kids! Let's look fresh for those other teams," I tell them. Hmmm…I wonder if my little honey is here. Pat and a volunteer turn us around, headed to go back out on the trail again. Guess the end of this race isn't in sight yet. Oh, looky there….My little girl is right across the trail I give her that wink and wag she likes so much. Pat has Tipper out of the sled and soon is taking care of our paws, looking for sore spots while applying that warm salve. We all get some refreshing water and a nice meal. I feel a good nap coming on. Pat is talking to Tipper and I think I know what it's about. He is going to have to take him out due to his sore wrist. When Pat takes him from the team, Tipper starts to put up a fight. He doesn't want to be taken away from the team. Tipper gets it. He's learned how important the team is and what an honor it is to be chosen to be part of it. I bark out to Tipper, "It's OK. Go with Pat. You've done a great job". Tipper walks off with his head down in shame. "Keep your head up Tipper, you're still part of our team. The effort that you've shown us will keep us going when the going gets tough. Thanks Tipper". I see Tipper look back with a smile as he lifts his head and proudly walks to the pickup.

I too have taken that walk and I don't plan it ever happening again. My wrist is sore, but I will not show pain, or limp. I will lead this team to the finish line. I just have to. Pat has leaders that are faster than me, but there is a reason that he put me up front and I know why. This race is going to get tougher before it gets easier and he wants someone with the mental toughness to lead this young team and Pat and I trust each other. I'm not getting any younger and this may be my last chance as a leader in a big race, and I plan to make the best of it. I'd better get some rest if I want to back-up my words. Pat is back and the soft sounds of humans talking put us all to sleep.

Another team preparing to leave wakes us up and as the team heads up onto the trail right near us. Pudges and I swing our team out onto the trail. Pat is telling us to settle down. What the heck! Are we in a race or what? He tells us we need some more rest and he is probably right. We head back to our nests and are out like a light. This happens two more times as our team is looking better each time. Elizabeth is still not herself and Pat is picking up some badly needed sleep. I start dreaming of nice fresh snow on my face while we are running full speed downhill. Pudges wakes me up and tells me to roll on my other side. I was running in my sleep on my side and I was kicking her. Just like a woman. Pat told me once that he couldn't get any sleep because Lisa kept waking him asking him to roll over on his side because he was snoring too loud. Now I understand what he was talking about. Wait a minute, that's snow, real snow. Pat is up and headed over to the log building. "AAR, AAR, Hey Pat, it's starting to snow real hard now." Moments later he comes back smelling of all kinds of human food. I've tried some of his human food, but I'd prefer a fatty chunk of meat any day.

Pat begins to massage our ankles once more and boy does that feel good. He walks Lady around. She is covering up her discomfort. As they walk by, she tells me not to say a word about her wrist to Pat. After some fresh snacks and some water, Pat sits down beside me. As he strokes my face, he tells of his concern about Lady. I look at Lady and I can tell how badly she wants to finish the race. I don't give him any signs. "If we make the wrong choice Casper, we'll be packing her a long ways," Pat tells me. I still don't let on to what I know. "OK Lady, you get to go on. Just give us your best, that's all I ask." Lady lets out a big sigh of relief and is very happy. "I won't let you guys down", she tells us. Lady gives me a smile of appreciation. "OK, everyone, let's fire up."

Pat:

When I pull the snow hook the team starts slowly, loosening up stiff muscles. Lady is pulling but still has a hitch in her step. We work our way up the trail…a couple of miles and her head is starting to bob a bit. I know then that she won't make it all the way to Pilgrim Creek. We'll have to pack her at some point. Mad at myself about not leaving her at the checkpoint, I hide my feelings because I don't want it to affect the morale of the team. Since we are only a couple of miles out I decide to turn the team around and go back to Four Corners to take her out of the team. If they don't want to leave the checkpoint again, I'll wait for Trent and his team to leave, and follow them out. It is one of those decisions you hope you'll never have to make.

I walk up to Lady, and tell her, "I'm sorry", and call Casper to "Haw, wheel around". Casper looks back up the trail in disbelief. "Casper, wheel around!" He gives me a stern look and begins to wheel the team around. I'm in the center of the team, holding the back six dogs in position until the front four get by, then I run back to the sled, turn around.... only to see Casper has turned them back up the trail again. "No, Casper". I walk back up and try it again. Once again Casper pulls the same trick. I want to get upset, but how can I get mad at the team's determination to continue? This time I stay on the sled and call out to Casper to "Wheel Around!" No one on the team even flinches. They are staring straight up the trail. WOW. There is a mutiny going on! I am stunned.

The team probably thinks I am going to get mad as hell, so instead, I let out a big laugh. They turn around, look at me and wag their tails. "OK, you guys, if this is the way you want it, I'm with you. Team Hup," I command. They lunge into their tugs and we are off again. So much for that idea, "Hey, Casper." as he looks back I tell him, "I don't appreciate you not listening to me, but that was the coolest damn thing any team of mine has ever done. Take us to the finish line Casper. He gives me a broad smile and turns his focus back to the trail ahead of him.

It's getting dark and snowing hard. We are just plodding along on this long uphill pull through 3 to 4 inches of fresh new snow. I am leaning on the handlebars and pumping one leg on the snow while the other leg rests on the runner. When one leg was about to give out, I would switch over to the other side of the sled and peddle with my other leg. We're all getting into a slow methodic rhythm. While we are plodding along this long uphill climb, I get this bad feeling that I may have screwed up trying to turn them around. Could I have broken their spirit, or do they still have that determined attitude to finish? I find myself in deep thought of how badly I want to finish this race. We haven't raced for the last three seasons and I know how long an off season can be when you have all year to think what you could have done better. I look up to see Lady working, although she is on only three and a half legs. I wish we could just catch a break. These guys deserve it.

Soon I find myself saying the "Hail Mary", a prayer that I learned as a small child, taught in Catholic schooling. It is a short prayer, and as soon as I finish it, I start to say it again. It becomes a slow chant. I know that I say it at least 15 times but it may have been over 50 times. I don't remember. All of a sudden I notice that my kicks are further apart. We are going faster. My God, we are at the top of the rise! The last time I consciously remember, we were only half way up the climb. Wow, this is great. The dogs are sharing my happiness as we start the long gentle drop down to the flats. It is so quiet and beautiful with the snow coming down into the light beam of the headlamp. It is one of those moments when you are reminded as to why you put yourself through all of this work, 24/7, 365.

What just happened? Did the team get lost in the prayer too? Did they just put one stride in front of the other out of habit, or was that some kind a small moment of divine intervention? I know but one thing. We are still moving, with about 23 miles of relatively mild trail ahead of us. I just hope the snow doesn't keep coming down like this.

I start to do the math in my head as if Trent left an hour after us. If we are lucky, he will pass us with his Iditarod team, just prior to the big climb. Then they would have to break the trail for the climb. I believe that we are going to be giving Lady a ride before we get there, so the sight of his team would be a good thing indeed. I keep the speed down so Lady can keep up with the healthy nine dogs that we have. Oh great, the snow is turning into slushy rain as we drop altitude. I don't ask myself, "What's next?" I don't even want to know!

Casper:

Pat gives the command to head out. The only problem is our mind say go but our muscles are still tight. We're out of sync. "Come on, you guys, let's get some rhythm going." Lady isn't looking good but isn't complaining. Her tug is tight. Our muscles are slowly loosening when Pat stops us, walks up to Lady and says he's sorry! Then, does the unthinkable and gives me the command to swing the team and head back to the checkpoint! I can't believe my ears. He says it again and out of instinct I start to turn us back. As Pat heads back to the sled, I do something I have never done before. I disobey my buddy. I turn the team back up the trail! I get the team lined back out but the snow hook is still set, holding us back. I'm afraid Pat is going to get mad. Instead he tells me that we have to take Lady back. "Lady, are you OK to go on? Be honest." "I have a lot more in me Casper", she answers. Pat gives me the "Wheel around Casper", command. I start it again but as we head back alongside the team I see that they look confused and defeated. I'm sorry, Pat, but this time I know better. I swing the team back up the trail and as the snow hook catches I begin to bark to let us go. He tries to get us to turn us around from the sled but I just stand there and look straight ahead. Nobody is moving a muscle. I'm concerned that Pat might have to shame me with a good scolding but instead, God love him, he lets out a roar of laughter. I'm shocked and the whole team is waiting to see how I am going to react. What the heck. I join in the laughter and the whole team starts in. The whole mood instantly lightens up. We are awake now and loosened up. I think to myself how cool that was, and how well Pat handled it. I swear, right then Pat tells me that was the coolest things he has ever seen any of his dogs do. This is getting weird. Pat and I are starting to think alike.

Pat:

The weather continues to be a menace. The wet snow has turned to slushy rain. I have been switching my hands back and forth on the handle bars but the gloves are now soaked through. Remember my favorite pair of gloves that I couldn't find back at

Pilgrim Creek? Well I still haven't figured out where they went and I'm paying for it now. I lost a glove once on a cold training run, while turning the team around in deep powder. I said then that I would always carry an extra pair of gloves. I remember the two sets of gloves back home, clench my hand into a fist.... water runs through my fingers. Why did I grab the pair of leathers? What a stupid move. I decide I am better off without them. I'll have to try to get them dried out again at Pilgrim Creek.

We have gone another twenty miles and are entering into a section of rolling trail, just prior to a steep climb. I stop the team, put some warming salve on Lady's wrist and apply a wrist wrap. I have a moment hugging Lady, thanking her for the unbelievable effort she has shown. The short downhill runs and punchy trail has finally taken its' toll on Lady's wrist. I pick her up and carry her back to the sled and gently place her in the spot I have prepared. As any good sled dog, she doesn't want to ride. I have to give her a couple of gentle taps on her nose, along with a very serious "NO", as she tries to jump out. She finally accepts her ride, but I have to let her head stick out of the bag so she can see what is going on.

"Well, guys, there it is, Whoa," as the team comes to a stop. Must be somewhere around 3 or 4 miles to the top of that climb. It starts about 100 feet ahead of us. I dig out the treat bag. Tails are wagging. Everyone gets a couple of different meat treats. It's time to jack this team up. I let out a couple of whoops and call out each dog's name as we head out. By the time we get around the first corner, the team is down to a slow walk. I can see this climb is going to be brutal.

Lady turns her attention from what's ahead, to what's behind us. It doesn't sink in with me why, until I see a faint flash of light and the whole team looks back. Is it just my wishful thinking, or was that the flash of a headlamp? My God, there it is again. It's Trent and his team. I am so grateful to see him that I about break into tears. They look steady as they approach us. I just say "Hi" as they go by, because I don't want to distract his dogs and break their climbing rhythm.

I could have kissed that man as he went by. That is saying a lot. You see, Trent has a huge red beard that reminds me of the TV commercial with the birds flying out of the guy's beard.

In all the miles of this racecourse, I could not have picked a more perfect place for a team to pass us. You see, if my team is competitive, they will want to draft or chase after a team when passed. "Hey, Casper, did you see all the good looking ladies?" I am playing him a bit, for Casper has a tendency to be what we call a "Horn Dog." They haven't met a team for a hundred miles and are ready for the chase! I let Trent get about 100 feet ahead, then pull the snow hook. Wow, feel that power! The dogs are churning up snow, trying to catch the team in front of them. In no time, Casper and Pudges are right up to the back of Trent's sled runners. Trent has us pass. I'm not sure whether he's going to snack his dogs or wants his dogs to draft off us up the climb. Without them in front, the team starts to slow down. Shortly Trent catches us and I tell him to go ahead. He has a little more speed and isn't packing a dog. As they pass, Lady decides she can't stand not be part of this....She goes wild and wants out. She could hurt herself so I reluctantly put her back in the team. A dog can pull uphill with this type of wrist injury, but can't run downhill on it. As soon as she is hooked in, she is barking and working up the whole team. We can't catch Trent but I don't let them know it. The dogs power, energy, and excitement, is affecting me. I am pumping and running as much as I can, but the snow is too soft to really help. The dogs are staying on top, but, if I try to step off the runners, I sink to my thighs. All I can do is encouraging them. And encourage I do. It is one of those moments where you realize you are witnessing a super dog team effort.

It is then that I realize this is my first race, where the whole team was born and raised in our kennel. I switched over from the Siberian-Malamute cross to the Alaskan Husky (mixed breed), years ago, when I purchased some breeding dogs from Terry Atkins and Butch Parr. At the time, Terry and his dogs had traveled more Iditarod miles than anyone. Butch had just won the tough 350 mile Race to the Sky in Montana. The male stud Ghost from Butch was via Joe Reddington's kennel (original organizer of the Iditarod Race), and that dog was bred with a daughter of 3 out of 4 Iditarod winning leader Elmer, of Doug Swingly's kennel. As the saying goes, "You can't make a race car out of go cart parts." An accomplished Iditarod musher once told me, that you can't make a winning team if you use your dogs on a guide team. They get a mind set of pulling weight, instead of running a fast racing pace. I can see how that can be true, but it doesn't diminish the heart or drive in a dog. This is what I am witnessing, right in front of me.

We are half-way up the mountain and the trail is firming up to where I can get off and run along side the sled. I am getting my second wind as well as the dogs. Even though we are tired and sore, we feel good. The strength is returning. I forget my age and replace it with an, "I can do it attitude." My heart feels like it is going to burst with pride. Rupert, Preacher, Panda, China, Patchy, Sheenje, Casper, Pudges, Snowy, and even Lady are powering it up the mountain. We are going to finish this race. I can't believe it as tears start to flow down my face. I'm totally caught up in the moment and overwhelmed by emotion, crying and laughing at the same time. The dogs must think I am loosing it, but I don't care. I am so proud of them and to be honest, I am proud of myself. Crazy as it might sound, I don't want the climb up this mountain, or this moment to ever end.

But it did. I see the top and am sad. I witnessed an effort by my dogs that many dog drivers never see. I work my way through the team, showering them with praise and attention. As I approach Lady to put her back in the sled, she lies down in the snow. She had given her all. I pick her up in my arms and give her kisses and love as I gently place her into the sled. She isn't resisting and it is the first time I have seen her so calm and content.

Casper:

The next section of the trail is a pleasure. Panda keeps trying to speed us up and I finally have to tell her to "knock it off." I have eight strong dogs behind me and Lady is keeping up, as long as we keep our speed down.

Once in a while one of the team will start giggling, remembering how funny Pat has behaved and soon the team is into a laughing fit all over again. Do you have any idea how hard it is to pull and laugh at the same time? I remind everyone to, "Save you strength, we have a steep climb coming up....We will have to work as a team like never before." The trail is starting to gently roll. My guess is that Pat will be put Lady in the sled soon. No sooner did I think that when Pat stops the team and lays Lady down in the sled bag. Ohhh, this is getting scarrrrrryyyy.

Lady isn't happy. I tell her "Don't worry about it. Let your wrist rest and the warm salve loosen it up. We've had lots of practice hauling all those humans around, so you'll be no problem." "Sorry, I've let you down" Lady says. I remind her that she is still part of the team and gave it her all, a great job. I don't think I convinced her.

At the base of the climb, and Pat brings us to a stop and gives us some warm snacks of sausage and starts this silly cheerleading thing. He's hopping all around clapping his hands and whooping it up. We're all looking at each other to see who's going to be the first to bust out laughing....I'm giving Pat a look that he is embarrassing himself, but he is into his antics so much he doesn't even notice me.

I wish I could tell him that the team understands the effort they will have to put out to get to the top. Soon the team is laughing again, even Lady. Then Pat runs back to the sled all excited and yells "HUP, HUP". I guess Pat got the reaction he wanted.

The steep climb quickly has us down to a slow walk, but the important thing is that we are moving. Everyone is doing their part.

"Do you hear that Casper? There's a team coming up behind us," Lady says from in the sled bag. Sure enough….there they are. This will perk the kids up, seeing another young team going up the steep grade. It's just the break we need!

As the team passes, Pat teases me about all the beauties going by….Don't worry, I see them. Lady wants out and I don't blame her. We've been waiting for a moment like this to prove how special we can be. I didn't think Pat would do it, but he hooks Lady back in the lines. He must know how important it is to her and is giving her the chance to shine. He is even thinking like a dog.

I can't repeat what she is barking. Her jumping up and down, cheers us up, and it fires up our engines good! Pat pulls the snow hook and before he can even give the command, we're off. In no time we're on the other musher's heels. The power in the team is infectious. We stop and let them get out ahead again, and again we catch them. We do this one more time and the other musher lets us pass. The only problem, once we pass, all of our young dogs keep looking back at the other team, breaking up the rhythm. Pat and the other dog driver are talking. Pat has us stop and let them pass. I tell the team, "OK you guys, it's time to become one." "What are you talking about Casper?" Patchy asks. "You know how Pat talks about being a team, or working as one? Well, I like to take it one step further. I like to picture us all becoming one, as if we are but one big dog. Of course, I'm the head. The sled is the belly. Lady, you might be the heart. Each one of you is a part. During the race you may even be different parts at different times." Sheenje then asks, "What part would Pat be, Casper?" "What part do you think he should be Sheenje?" I ask. I could tell by the chuckles that some of them had an idea of what part Pat might be, remembering all the flatulation noises he made earlier that morning. Sheenje says, "I think he is the beautiful hide that holds us all together." "I agree Sheenje, that's how I see him too!"

Pat says "HUP" and we all hit our tug lines. Moving as one…one big dog, is incredible! The team feels it, and Pat feels it too. Do you remember earlier, when I talked about how we have the ability to feel, what Pat is feeling through the lines? Well, I think this is the first time Pat has felt what we are experiencing and it sure feels good!

Our effort builds as we climb. The "One" dog seems bigger and more powerful. A wave of confidence overcomes us. Nothing will stop us. When I look back through the team, I am almost overcome with pride and just about to break into tears when I realize Pat already has. He can be such a mess. The top half of this mountain is ours. We quietly share this special moment.

As we hit the rise of the ridge, we are all congratulating each other. Lady lies down. She has given her all. Pat comes up and lovingly carries her back to the sled for her ride into the next rest stop. The really neat thing was that as Pat carried her by the rest of the team, they all could see that she had a smile from ear to ear. She finished on her terms.

Treats and lots of loving' are on the menu before we continue. Pat gives me a look that I will never forget. All he said was "Thanks Casper". "You're welcome Pat," is all I say. We share a simple smile and go back to work. Life is good…

WE'RE GOING TO FINISH THIS RACE

Off Fons Butte and Pilgrim Creek Checkpoint

Pat:

The kids are in a jovial mood as we prepare to head down off the ridge. Of course, they all want to run and stretch, even Casper. Lady settles in for her ride as I pull the snow hook. We take off at a dash. This is fun, winding around the corners with my foot on the drag brake. When we approach a wide corner with a steep bluff, Lady pops her head out to take a look. As I reach down to give her a calming pat on her head, she reaches up with her paw, to say thanks, and pulls apart the wiring to my headlamp. Everything turns pitch black! Wow! Talk about excitement! I apply the main brake with all my weight and I grab for Lady. I lean hard right into the mountainside, trying my best to stay away from the bluff to my left. We slowly come to a stop. I'm frantically trying to match the terminals of wiring back together before the team takes off again. The light pops back on! My God, we have stopped right on the edge of the bluff! Nothing like a little extra excitement! Giddy with relief, I gain control of my heartbeat. The dogs are looking at me like I'm a bonehead.

The last few miles of the ride into the Pilgrim Creek Checkpoint are, thankfully, uneventful. Panda hasn't been pulling her tug lineShe's has been going 110% since the beginning of the race! She is young and hasn't learned to pace herself. By the time we arrive I decide to drop Lady and Panda. I don't want to take the chance of making the last leg of the race tougher by possibly having to pack Panda in the sled. With some considerable extra time, I could keep Panda in the team... Instead, I give the team a little extra rest, and we could finish before daylight. Then I'd have time to take the snowmobile out and groom the fresh snow for the sprint teams run on Sunday. I would sure like to be there to support Lisa for Sunday's events. We will start out with eight strong dogs for the final 25.4 miles to the finish line.

There is a gentle snowfall as we approach the checkpoint. The bonfire ahead is a sight for tired eyes. The glow sticks don't affect the team as Casper swings us into and through the woods. I stop the team prior to our rest spot and take Lady out of the sled bag and walk with her to the parking lot where my trailer is available for dropped dogs. Lady is happy to see her box and jumps right in. I apply some warming salve to her wrist as she settles in for a nice nap. Shortly I return with Panda. Both receive lots of lovin', praise, water and snacks. I tell them that I will see them tomorrow morning at the finish. Neither dog seems sad to be taken out of the race... they are proud that they have done their best. We head to the same spot where we rested when on the outbound trail.

Once again, dog care comes before anything else. The dogs are tired and grateful for all the attention. They are probably hoping that dirt and rocks that we went over on the out going trail are now covered in snow. Little do they know that section of trail for the return trip to the start-finish line, has been thrown out of the race. I'm content and relaxed working with the dogs. The dogs sense this and settle into a well-deserved nap.

Casper:

The trek down into our last checkpoint is almost uneventful. Things are going nicely, until Pat, for some odd reason, turns his light off! We like to run in the dark, but I know Pat is blinded by it. By the time I get the team to a stop, we can feel Pat's racing heartbeat through the lines. I don't know why he turned his light off. Unless there is still a streak of thrill searcher left in the old fart. Just when I think I have him figured out, he pulls something like that. We can't figure out if he did that as a joke or if he is just a bonehead. He needs to quit goofing off and get us to our rest spot.

Pudges and I gently lead Pat through the trees, past the big hole that Pat had all the fun going into last time we passed here. He stops us short of our rest spot to take Lady and Panda from the team. Panda seems a bit surprised and disappointed. When she gets to the trailer and looks back, I give her a well-deserved wink and smile for a job well done. She smiles back as she settles into her nest. Shortly the team is falling asleep to Pat's gentle touch on our wrists, feet, neck and back. The last I remember is listening to Pat's humming of a simple soothing song and thinking to myself, "Yeah Baby, We're Gonna Finish This Race".

Pat:

I've never enjoyed massaging my dogs as much as I am now. The dogs are melting in my hands with total trust. They know what I know. We are going to finish this race. We share this relaxed state. I sit on the snow with them and for the first time in my life I feel as though I am one of them.

The moment reminds me of my first race in Montana, sitting on a ridge, resting the dogs under a full moon. It was there while lying in the sled that I realized that driving a dog team is something that has more reality in it than anything that I had ever done before. For some reason I knew those dogs lined out in front of me, held the keys to a lot of doors in my life. They have not only opened many doors of opportunity, but also the doors that have opened me up, teaching me to be a better person. The dogs identify your weaknesses. Work to lessen your weaknesses, or go down with the team. I have failed at many races in my lifetime. But over time, by working on my own weaknesses, we have learned to triumph over adversity. I owe much to them. They have helped mold me into the person that I have become. One of the most blessed things that ever have happened to me is that I have found the person to spend the rest of my life with. Lisa understands that the dogs are part of the reason that I am the person that she has fallen in love with. I in turn, love her even more for that.

As I sit here, it is wonderful, knowing I am now, one of them. I will savor this moment for a lifetime.

After sitting there for some time, my stomach growls. The dogs are all asleep, so I slip off to the warming hut to have a bite to eat. Along the way I place my rain soaked leather gloves in the warmth of the open fire pit. The smell of all the fine foods hit me in the nose as we enter the warming hut. I tried everything there, including some seconds. Mary comes in and I jump out of my seat, I tell her I owe her a real hug from the last time we came through here. She accepts my offer and everyone seems pleased that I am back to my old self.

My boots and socks are off and my feet feel good in the warmth of the log cabin. Others probably don't appreciate me drying my socks on the edge of the stove, but no one says anything. Out of the clear blue, the plastic strips in the doorway, are parted by a pair of crutches! It's Steve, fresh cast and all. We are shocked to see him, only hours after he had pins put in his ankle. I express to him my feeling bad of his misfortune. I ask him now that he has seen Katie's dog team, "Do you think you could have won this race? He tells me, "I'm sure I could have won it." I don't tell him that I believe Katie's team has a lot more in their tank. She could have knocked off a few more hours off their time had they been really pushed by another team. I could be wrong. It would be interesting to see them race against each other in the future. It isn't long and Steve heads outside to have his drop bags put in his truck.

The vets finish giving an IV to a dog from a team that came in ahead of us. We are getting a chuckle as to how well Trent is sleeping through all of the noise. Out of nowhere, Erica (the vet with the lovely New Zealand accent) says, "Now that you've eaten well and are hydrated, you are going outside with me and I am going to take you to bed!" Of course she is talking to the dog she has been working on, but if you know me, you know I can't pass this one up. I tell her, "Well I'm really flattered, but I think Lisa might have something to say about that!" There is dead silence until everyone bursts into laughter. I tell them that they don't have to laugh that hard. That made them laugh even harder.

Hey, I'm back. If I'm not trying to be funny, then I am not myself. Sure feels good to hear people laugh. My head drops and I fall into a deep sleep. Trent and I proceed to sawing lots of logs together with our chorus of snoring.

Later I hear Trent putting on his boots. As he heads out, I remember a dream that I often have. An Iditarod team is leaving ahead of me from Pilgrim Creek to the finish line. The snow is falling so they are breaking trail. A third of the way, we start to see the tracks of the sled ahead of us. We finally have them in sight as we start up Palmeroy Ridge and we overtake them just before the top and then race downhill into the finish line with the other team on our tails.

It's my turn to boot up and I can hardly move! My age and previous miles have caught up with me. While pulling my boots on, with my fingers cracked and bleeding, I remember that I left my gloves by the fire. When I got there, someone kind had turned them over and they are completely dry. That perks me up. I put some salve on my hands so that I can use them without being in too much pain. I check my watch and see that we can leave again soon.

RACE TO THE FINISH LINE

From Pilgrim Creek Checkpoint to the Finish Line

Casper:

I hear the familiar sound of Pat pulling out treats for eats. Hey; "Treats for eats. I'm a poet and never even knowed it. Ha, Ha." That was a great nap. The rest of the team is stretching and taking care of business. Pat is moving better. He sure looked old when I woke up earlier and saw him hunched over. Everyone is really quiet as Pat puts our booties on. We know there's a long section of trail to finish but by the looks of it, they all want to finish it just as bad as Pat I want to finish.

We are confident but not cocky - absolutely determined to see the finish. I don't have to do any cheerleading. These pups have grown up right in front of Pat and me. Some humans come to guide us back out but we just pass them after Pat pulls the snowhook and tells them that we are fine. We wind our way out of the woods back onto the main trail. Pudges isn't keeping the line tight and it's disrupting our rhythm so Pat stops us and calmly brings Sheenje into lead and takes Pudges back to her spot. We try it again, but Sheenje is uncomfortable leading in such a big race. Pat notices how her tail is tucked between her legs, so he switches her out and puts big Preacher in lead. Preacher just looks at me and says, "Hold on for the ride big boy". Wow, I had never seen that look in her eyes. In fact, it's kind of turning me on. Pat must have seen my admiration and scolds, "Cool your jets, straight ahead Casper." "Sorry Pat, I was a little, caught up in the moment". Preacher is powering into her harness and before long the whole team is into the steady, mild climb away from the rest area.

We approach the split in the trail. If we go Gee, it's back over that climb. If we go Haw, it's back to where the race started. Pat calls "Haw", I instantly turn the team Haw, to the finish. The snow's coming down as we're cutting through fresh snow. A little further I see the tracks of the sled in front of us. I line us up so that Pat can keep our sled on the tracks in front of us. The sled is moving easier and we begin to gain speed, feeding off the building energy that Pat is sending through the lines. A little further is the next split in the trail. Haw, takes us onto that trail that had the exposed dirt and rocks towards the ski park. To all our surprise, Pat calls out "Gee". We are headed on a straight shot to the finish line. The team, (I won't call them kids anymore) is elated and shift up a gear. Around the next corner, there are dog tracks in the snow. Are we gaining on them? All I know is the tracks are fresher. Pat is whooping it up. We are gaining on that team in front of us. The chase is on!

Pat:

The snow continues to fall. I wonder if it's slowing down Trent's Iditarod team ahead of us. I remember my dream as I bootie up the team. There's no need to cheer this team up to leave. They are ready and to finish this race. Volunteers come over to help us wind our way through the timber and back on to the main trail and I tell them, "Thanks, but my leaders have it." When we hit the trail I can see that Pudges is slow starting, so I stop move Sheenje up into her spot. Sheenje has her tail between her legs, so I take her out and place Preacher in lead. Years ago, I would have freaked out by now, but I remember watching the first winner of this race from years ago, go through the same thing with his leaders. He was so patient with them. It seemed as though he went through his whole team before he had the right combination. I have heard from more experienced mushers than I, say, "That the right combination is always within the team for each situation. The trick is in the right combination!" Preacher presses into her harness and we are off.

We take the left fork back to the finish line and there they are, in the snow. Is my dream coming true? Sled tracks! We're catching up. Maybe I am just imagining that we are catching up. I steer our sled onto the polished sled tracks stretched out in front of us and our speed increases. I begin pedaling my outside leg like I'm some young dog driver, trying not to get too excited.

At the next split in the trail, I know the dogs are thinking we'll head back to the ski park. I surprise them with a last moment to call them to the right, "Gee". The team happily swings the team past Ski Park Road. Now we only have a couple of hours to finish. The dogs are getting excited, and then I see why. Dog tracks in the snow! Damn, we are gaining on them. I am ecstatic. My dream is coming true. We have a reputation to uphold, that Dogsled Express always races right to the finish line. "OK Team, Let's go get'em."

Casper:

Man, this is beautiful. The snow has let up as a cold wind blows sideways across the trail. The cold wind is refreshing as a cold drink of spring water, especially after running through all the warm spots along race course.

I wish we could have run this race two years ago. It was cold. I heard a human say it was 8 degrees below zero, what ever that means, it was perfect traveling weather for us dogs. Pat just stood around and watched all day and night. We all felt kinda cheated that year, although it was fun running around the short track with that young lady Ashley, driving. I don't understand why someone would do all that training just run around that little loop. It was fun to see Lisa head out in the four dog race, with Pat's old leaders Kissy and BoBo. Forget about feeling Lisa's energy through the lines. We could feel it from inside the trailer. She was shaking like a leaf when she left and calm as a sleeping puppy when she returned. I heard her say how much fun it was to pass her friend Kathy. I guess she has a competitive streak in her, after all!

The snow is turning colder, making the trail faster and easier to run on! I imagine that Pat, like me, will always wonder what this race could have been if we had a cold solid trail like this the whole race. Tipper, Lady and Panda wrists would be fine and would still be in the team. Pat would have been able to let us compete instead of it becoming a race of mental fortitude.

"HUP, HUP Casper" Pat startles me out of thinking about what may have been. Pat is having too much fun, acting like a kid racing his bicycle to a candy store. It's great to see after all we have been through the last 165 miles. The others have picked up on it too. Everyone is chasing the fresh tracks that seem to come and go with the blowing winds.

I am, in turn, in no hurry. You see, I don't want this race to finish!! I've raced up north where we had the second fastest team on a tough 220 mile course and Pat even won the Veterinarian's award and the Sportsmanship Award. We started and finished with 12 dogs that race. It was almost the perfect race, but not nearly as rewarding as this.

You see, any dog can lead a team when things are going well. Only a few can keep things going when things go to hell in a hand basket. I am proud of myself and proud of my dear friend Pat. If all of this adversity had happened a few years ago, I don't know if we could have kept it all together. I don't know how many more of these long races I have left in me. This is my moment and I don't want it to end. Preacher scolds, "To pick it up." I shouldn't be so selfish. I lean into a strong pull and never share my thoughts with the others because everyone is having so much fun being a part of the chase. I bark out to the others, "OK YOU SLED DOGS EXTRAORDINARE, IT'S TIME TO MAKE OUR MOVE."

It's like magic. As we cross the flats were are moving as one smooth big dog. I savor every step. I can barely see the outline of the Mother Mountain to our left. The stars momentarily pop in and out of the clouds. The moment finally overwhelms me. Everyone and everything turns quite. The soft beautiful sounds of Pat and us breathing as one and the high notes created by the runners gliding over the cold snow. It's, " The Song of the Runners", chorused by the jingles of our snaps touching our collar rings. Our spirit dog, Sheenje, softly whispers. "Are you OK Casper"? After a few moments all can I manage to say is, "I have never been better. Thanks, you guys."

The distant sound of Pat's snowmobile, soon breaks the silence. Man, I hate those things.

A few years back, while giving a ride to an elderly couple, we had some young guys go flying by us on their snowmobiles. They yelled back "You sure are slow." We were mad at them and Pat was quietly upset. On the way back we come around a corner and there are the same two snowmobiles, moving slowly. One machine was pulling the other. Pat hikes us up, and we pass at a full lope. As we passed them, Pat said, "But we don't ever break down", followed by his belly filled roar of laughter. The passengers and team joined in. It was great. What a character.

We head to the left as the snowmobile passes us on the right.

Pat:

This is just too much fun. Moments like this are why I run dogs. We're in perfect rhythm. I shut my light off. I can barely make out the form of the dogs. As we roll over the short humps in the trail, moving as one body, like we are one. I am lost in the flowing motion of the team.

Dog tracks, looking really fresh, jolt me back from my revelry. I look up ahead... swear that was the flash of a headlamp. If it was Trent's, they must be above the switchback, only a mile or less ahead of us. My God, is my dream actually going to happen? I take off running till I can run no more. Then I peddle until I can't peddle anymore. Soon I hear my snowmobile with Race Marshal, Bill. He passes to the right as we continue the chase. Just before we get to that switchback that scared me so bad a day and a half ago, I see where the snowmobile tracks head straight up the bank and don't come back down. The dogs are looking up the hill and out of the dark, I here Bill's voice. "Beautiful night, isn't it Pat?" "It sure is Bill." I don't shine my light too close for I don't want to interrupt what may be only his business, if you know what I mean. "What are you up to Bill", I ask. He tells me that he was enjoying listening to me come up the trail while I talked to my dogs. He likes this quiet spot, amongst the big trees. "I think I'll take a little nap here before I head into the finish line," he tells me. "Sounds good to me Bill, and thanks for the nice job, we really appreciate your help" and I grab the snowhook to leave. "HEY Pat." he shouts as I release the brake. I stop the team. "Great race" Bill says. "Would have been a lot better if those rains hadn't hit," I say. "Don't worry about it, the return trip is great. I've seen worst. You just have to go with the flow. Beautiful country you have." "Thanks Bill, I needed that. Have good dreams and see you at the finish line." It's only a few miles to the open view of the whole drainage. If the other team is ahead, we should see them soon.

It's a good time to contemplate the team. Casper-----What can I say? We did it buddy. Preacher-----The one that I knew had the skills... but did she have the drive? I don't have to worry about that anymore! China-----The quiet one, that does her job without directing any attention to herself. Snowy-----The last time, she got over excited and it zapped her strength so I had to pull her out of the race early. She has proven that she has learned how to pace herself, while staying in the tug the whole time. Patchy-----The young dog, that I never had to say a word to. The constant worker. Next year she has a shot as leader. Sheenje-----The spiritual leader of the team. A joy to start and finish the race with. My little girl. Pudges-----Casper kind of wore her down due to his size, pulling her back and forth, looking for the best part of the trail. Now that she has a break from him she is hard at it. She has always done whatever I have asked of her. A special dog. Rupert------What a wonderful surprise. I never know what he is thinking. I thought of not running him in this race due to his tendency to turn around at inappropriate times. He didn't even consider it when I tried to turn the team back at Four Corners. Look at you! You are outworking all the other dogs on the team. I never would have guessed that you could put out like this. Well done Rupert.

I now understand why Terry Atkins says, "Give me eight great dogs and I will go anywhere with them." I have eight great dogs in front of me. They have grown up as a team right before my eyes. With a good rest, I could count on them to get up and continue on. Jack told me that some teams don't kick into gear until they hit over a hundred and fifty miles. I have seen it before and I am seeing it again today. What a joy. I will never forget this race. I have had better races by the finish standings, but never a more satisfying experience.

Daylight approaches as we round the corner. The whole drainage is in view. I don't see Trent and his dogs. They could be behind that pocket of timber about half way up. His young team could shut down near the top of this five mile climb. We race for two reasons. It's in our character, and it's just plain fun. I see us all as one big dog.

Casper:

A short ways up the trail we smell the man on the snowmachine. We could let Pat know, but choose not to, due to his wonderful calmness. The man is sitting there in the dark above us. Pat gives us the command to stop. It is nice to listen to these good men. There is great respect between them. There is even a non-spoken communication. It is short lived. You see most humans have lost their ability to communicate without spoken words. It's too bad. There is so much we could teach and share with each other.

When we head up the trail, Pat lets out a huge sigh of relief. What ever that man told him, sure relaxed him. His worries are lifting from him, and I'm happy for him.

Just around the big corner Pat turns his headlight off. He says he doesn't want the team in front, to see us coming. I didn't have the heart to tell everyone that by the calculations of my nose, that team is already over that pass ahead of us. They're having so much fun, and I don't want to take that away from them.

Pat continues to praise our efforts as we near Pomeroy Ridge. I'm sorry, but it's not cheering me up. The closer we get to the ridge the closer it is to my job being over. This has been the most challenging set of circumstances I have ever been in charge of, but also the most rewarding. I look back at the team and Pat. They are all beaming with pride, as they should be. Pat must have sensed my somberness. He shouts out, "Hey everybody, how about the job Casper has done? Join me with three cheers for Casper. HUP HUP HOORRAY, HUP HUP HOORAY, HUP HUP HOORAY". I have to admit it helps me get out of blues along with all the nice things my teammates say to me. What they told me, is between them and me.

The flat of the ridge is right before us. Pat starts to whoop it up like he always does when the last climb is over and it is smooth going to the finish line. He sounds like half man and half dog. The team joins in. He stops us at the top and brings out the rest of the meat treats. We pig out. Our bellies feel so warm and full. Pat kneels down to me, wraps his arms around my neck, and breaks down in tears. "We did it, Casper. We did it." was all he could say. After a while he gets up and as he walks away he stops, turns around, comes back and whispers in my ear so the others can't hear, "I picked the right dog for the job, Casper. Thank You."

That's it, I have to look away or I won't able to see through my own tears for the fun- run down the mountain to the finish line.

Pat:

When I realize that my vision of us catching an Iditarod team was only a dream, sinks in about a mile from the top of Polmeroy Ridge, I think....that's OK. This has been quite the ride!

Remembering the start of the race when wondering what I will learn about myself or of the dogs from this race, I ponder as we work our way up to the ridge.

We have run more physically difficult races, but then I was both mentally and physically rested. I was both physically and mentally spent, when this race started! Knowing how I handled racing under this kind state of stress and I can see how these skills may serve me later in life. What a great feeling.

The sunlight peeks over the far ridge to the east as we approach the pass. Everyone is feeling good except Casper. His ears are laid back and down. He doesn't wag his tail when I speak to him. Is Casper is feeling how I did as we approached the top of Fons Butte? Maybe, Casper doesn't want the race to end either.

I lead the team in a cheer and a nice song for Casper, to perk him up. He responds with a smile and a slow twirl of his tail as we approach the top of Pomeroy Pass. When reaching the top everyone enjoys the moment as I pass out the remaining treats and praise each and every dog. When I get to Casper I loose it. I don't know how long I knelt there and held him. As I head back to the sled I paused, go back to him and whisper a little something in his ear. Casper is now standing at attention, leaning hard into his harness, ears up, tail a wagging, and ready to go. "Hey Casper, what do you say we have some fun on this downhill run to the finish."

We take off! In a flash they are in the groove, working our way to the finish line. In every race, I have a flashback when I was a little kid on the baseball mound. Dad was at the game. Normally I am striking batters out right and left. This game they were hitting everything thrown at them. I wanted the coach to replace me, but for some reason he was leaving me in through the inning. When the game was over, I could tell my Dad was upset with me. "You embarrassed yourself and me," he frowned. "They were hitting everything I threw at them Dad, I'm sorry." "I'm not mad because they were hitting your pitches… I don't give a damn about that. I'm mad because you thought about quitting on the mound. No kid of mine is a quitter." He told me he's going home and that I need to ride home with the team, not him. I felt awful. From that day on, I've always given my best to the last play of the game. I say a little prayer, thanking him for that valuable life lesson.

It's time for the goofy song again. I'm on a roll as the Irish tune is mixed with rap along with the same foul noises I used eighty miles ago. All tails are wagging… I'm even laughing at myself, so you know it's bad. With only a mile to go and there is a big hump of snow down the middle of the road. Out of the nowhere, Casper shoots us right over the top of it to the other side. "Ha Ha Casper, thought you were going to loose me Huh. Gotcha! Try it again buddy." I'll be damned if he doesn't shoot us over the top again. Still laughing, we approach the finish line. When we cross, there is no one in sight! This happened once before in Montana. It took three tries to finish that race. No one was there to greet me at the finish line. As before, I suspect that we came in a little sooner then figured.

Finally, I spot Lisa and call for her. She runs over and gives me a big hug and kiss. She looks exhausted as she tells me that Steve has a dog loose and she hasn't slept all night. I feel bad for her as she helps me put the dogs up in their boxes. Lisa asks if the team needs food and water and I tell her no, that I had recently feed them four miles out. What they need now is rest.

We work our way over to the warming hut and I change socks and have a bite to eat. Steve's dog shows up, so Lisa is feeling better.

Things have settled down a bit. Panda, Lady, Lizzy and Tipper have been brought back from the checkpoints by volunteers, so I walk them to our truck to join the team. I have them all out on their drop chains alongside the pickup. One by one I inspect each dog. Tipper's wrist is almost healed. Elizabeth is bouncing around, being herself again. Lady is sore but she is putting all her weight on her bad wrist. Panda is eating like a pig and looks her old self. I slowly help each dog into their own box as I shower the team with love and praise. I leave Casper to last. "Casper, I don't think I should try to compete in another two hundred mile race, while being the race organizer. With the business and all, we may never be able to run a two hundred mile race again together." Casper's ears drop. "How about we have an open class so we can run a shorter distance with more dogs on a team? We have some young fast leaders coming up. Could you be happy running back in the team and not in lead all the time?" Well I don't think I have ever seen Casper so happy. He was spinning and jumping around on three legs. I see that he isn't putting all his weight on his front left leg. I reach down to check his wrist as he offers it to me. It is so stiff that I can barely fold it under. He winces but doesn't whimper. "You tough old son of a gun, how long have you been hiding this?" He looks up and gives a big old sly smile. "And by the way there buddy boy, when did you become such a jokester, taking me over those jumps in the last mile?" Casper jumps up and hits me in the nose with his nose. It's the true sign of affection, husky language.

"Casper, I didn't want this race to end either." His head snaps up and looks deep in my eyes. "We will always share this special bond. I will carry it with me forever. No one can take away what we have." I gently pick up my buddy and place him in his warm box. I look him straight in his eyes. "I love you Casper" and I close the door.

Casper:

Pat pulls the snow hook for the last time. We head for the finish line. It isn't long before Pat start that silly song again! By the time he starts faking body function noises again, we are a mess laughing! Since he is having so much fun I decide to pull one on him. I shoot us over the bump in the trail. I look back to see Pat all wide-eyed as he catches air. He lets out a bellowing laugh and dares me to do it again. He doesn't think I really will, so what the heck. He catches more air.

We cross the line and no one is in sight. Soon Lisa comes running and the two have a long awaited embrace. That's beautiful. I don't know who looks more tired, Pat or Lisa. They put us in our boxes and Pat whispers that he will be back as soon as things settle down. I wake to the sound of Pat hooking up Lady and Panda to the drop chains. We all get out for a stretch, water and snacks. I look under the pickup to the other side and see that Lizzy is back to her silly self and Tipper is bouncing around on his bad wrist stealing Lizzy's food. Pat takes his time inspecting each dog and gives good words and soft strokes before putting us in our boxes.

He turns to look at me. First he tells me that he doesn't think we'll ever run another two hundred mile race together again. I am instantly shocked. I can't believe it. Is he quitting racing? Then he wants to know what I think about running a shorter open class, with me in the team, letting the younger faster dogs run in lead. Well, hell yeah. I'm for all of that. Pat notices I don't have all my weight on a front foot as I jump in excitement of his idea. As he lovingly inspects my wrist he shakes his head back in forth in disbelief. I almost pulled it off, as I give him a sheepish smile. Next, he wants to know where the jokester in me came from, sending him into the air like that. Well, where do you think you bonehead? I learned from a master. Master Pat!

To this day I can't believe what he said next. He tells me he didn't want the race to finish either! Had he been reading my mind? Maybe Pat is learning again, the language of no words.

He then, talks about the bond we will share for life, and tells me, that he loves me,   Pat closes the door and as he walks away, I whisper a message in my head to him. "I love you to Pat".

"I love you too Casper, and thank you." He heard me!

TWO EVENINGS LATER

At home

Pat:

Two days of good rest, and life starts to return to normal. The dogs are healthy and ready to go back to work tomorrow. The rest of the sprint races went well Sunday. I managed to get out with the groomer before they raced so that they had a freshly groomed trail.

The post race banquet was a lot of fun. Katie had a great race taking 1st place. Bino took second, and also won the Sportsmanship Award for stopping and sticking his snowhook in a crevice in the concrete wall, then running across the opposite side of the road to help Steve turn his team around after breaking his ankle. Chris, in his first distance race, was pleased with his 3rd place finish. Trent, took 4th place, a little over an hour ahead of us, also winning the prestigious Veterinarian's Award, for Best Cared Team. We won the Red Lantern Award and 5th place.

Chris had a wonderful surprise when his family showed up in the middle of the night to greet him at the finish line. His beautiful little daughter was so proud of her Daddy. I told her, "Your Daddy is a pretty tough guy to do that well in his first big race." She beamed with pride. I also told her that, "Your Daddy isn't a quitter, and you can always count on him to be there for you." She reached up and gave her Daddy a big hug around his waist. It was a moment when you realize all the hard work was worth it.

Oh, by the way. Do you remember those gloves I lost? Well, after the race, while Rick and I were breaking down the sled and gear, I found them underneath the sled bag, on top of the sled. They must have fallen down there when I had the sled on its' side, changing the runner covers. Rick tells me that he didn't give us even a fifty-fifty chance of finishing the race. I told him proudly, "I knew the team was tough... I just didn't know they were that tough".

The dogs are fed and it is almost dark. All in the kennel are nestled into their houses, except twelve dogs. You guessed it. The twelve I raced with. Their houses are all lined up in a row and they are all sitting on their haunches watching me. The race changed them. They have grown up. I say goodnight, leaving Casper last. I don't view Casper the same as I used to. He is much more than a good leader. He is my friend. I lead them in a good howl as I cross the bridge on the way back to the cabin.

Casper:

Pat has fed us well with our kibble and meats. The soreness in my wrist is gone and the rest of the team has healed up well. Lizzy keeps asking me questions about being a lead dog. She must believe I'm stupid, if she thinks I don't know what she is up to. She wants my job! I'll teach her all I can, for I want this kennel to hold its claim as a top distance team in California. I get such a kick out of saying that, because there are actually, only a handful of distance teams even in California! Pat gives the race team a special goodnight and heads back over to the log cabin. He stops in the middle of the bridge and lets out one of his long beautiful howls. The whole kennel sets off and joins in. I used to say that Pat is as close as he could be to being one of us when he leads us in song. Now I say, "When he leads us in that song, he is one of us." Song of the Runners

Goodnight my good friend.

THE END

Made in the USA
San Bernardino, CA
09 December 2013